WOW!
WHAT A RIDE!
A QUICK TRIP THROUGH EARLY SEMICONDUCTOR
AND PERSONAL COMPUTER DEVELOPMENT

GENE CARTER

Lulu Publishing Services rev. date: 04/04/2016

Dedication

To my wife Pat.

She stood by me and took care of our family while I followed
my dreams. I uprooted her and the family from a place she
loved – Albuquerque, New Mexico – and transported them
to California with the promise that we would stay just 5 years
to make whatever fame and fortune I could generate.

We are still there!

Contents

Preface

This is a story of how some of the greatest inventions of the mid–twentieth century were created. I had the good fortune to be a part of many of them. I have interspersed the book with some questions about how events happen. Are they created by fate or planning? This will add some philosophical theory to the events that I am recalling. Some of you will believe that fate doesn't exist while others will believe that someone or somehow, you are placed in life's situations by a higher being … your choice.

I chose the book title from a Hunter S. Thompson saying that describes my philosophy on life.

> *"Life should not be a journey to the grave with the intention of arriving safely in a pretty and well preserved body, but rather to skid in broadside in a cloud of smoke, thoroughly used up, totally worn out, and loudly proclaiming* "WOW, what a ride!!!"

Looking back, I realize how fortunate I was in my selection of life's journey. I was an average student in high school. Music and math were my favorite subjects. The rest of the classes … not so much. I wanted to be a professional musician but wasn't good enough to be among the best so I eventually chose electronics. I have had the opportunity to do so many things and experience so much while working with some of the best engineers and scientists of our times and want to share those experiences with you in layman's language.

Most people spend their entire life looking for the ultimate job. I was blessed with positions in four different environs: engineering, marketing, sales, and finally venture capital investing. This provided a variety of new experiences for learning and utilizing different skillsets. The stories told in this writing are not meant to be "earth shattering" events but merely to provide a look at behind the scenes incidents in some of the most exciting developments of the mid– twentieth century – all connected to the world of *semiconductors.*

In just fifty years, semiconductor technology changed the world of electronic communications. Computers, created using semiconductor technology, changed the way the world lives, works and communicates. Both discoveries created the connection of people worldwide, through a communication medium called the Internet. These technologies are on a par with developments that occurred during the industrial revolution with the invention of modern farm machinery, the automobile, and the airplane. These inventions changed manufacturing technology and the way we travel and work. Semiconductor technology changed the way we communicate. All of these innovations changed the way we live and work.

Some of the events covered in this publication touch on the very people that made these things happen. This is a look at the "behind the scenes" activities of some monumental technological developments that helped shape the twentieth century semiconductor and communications revolution. I hope you will enjoy reading about how this great technological advancement evolved through what I called **"Necessity is the mother of invention."** My adventures and narratives are related to their development.

Acknowledgment

I must give a special thanks to Jack and Pat Stewart for editing my book. Their support, guidance, and suggestions helped me immeasurably in its completion.

How it all began

To set the stage for these events, I must provide some background information that I think is relevant to how life transpired, so bear with me.

During my junior year in high school, the Korean War broke out and about half of the boys in our senior class belonged to the Air National Guard unit at Rosecrans Air Field in St. Joseph, Missouri. They were called up in February of 1951 before they graduated, and sent to France to replace an Air Force unit that was sent to Korea. That was a great awakening for several of us in the junior class. At 17, we joined the Naval Reserves rather than take the chance of being drafted into the Army. For me, this was the last choice, but not the best choice since I didn't like water. We graduated from high school in May 1952 and that summer we went to two weeks of boot camp at the Great Lakes, Illinois Naval Training Center in Chicago. That was a rude awakening for many of us. We were exposed to service discipline, unlike "mom" discipline, and definitely a different way of life.

The Navy determines the capabilities of new recruits using a battery of tests called the General Classification Test (GCT). These tests determined your aptitude and qualifications in a particular classification of job functions called "rates." There were two choices: the "deck apes" as we called them, that wore white rating stripes and worked in office jobs or deck handling jobs, and the "black gang" which were below-deck functions like electricians, boiler tenders, machinist mates, and electronics technicians. They wore red rating stripes. I had an interest in electrical engineering, even though I had no intention of going to college, and had a high enough GCT score to qualify for an electronics technician rating. Our training in the chosen rate began in the Naval Reserves every Monday night.

There was a shortage of electronics technicians and ET's were considered a critical rate. In 1956, there were rumors that Electronic Technicians on active reserve status were going to be recalled to active duty. Our reserve instructor had been in WWII and the Korean War and didn't want to go back on active duty so he quit the reserves and left us without an instructor. A few months later in November, I received notice that I was being drafted and ordered to report to the Army on January 6, 1957. Being a naval reservist, I was given the opportunity to report for active duty in the Navy the day before I was to report to the Army induction center. On January 5, 1957, I reported to the Navy induction center at Treasure Island in San Francisco, California.

I had the rate of fireman and if you are not a petty officer when you go aboard ship, you serve mess cook duty for several months – a fate worse than death for me. Needless to say, I panicked since I was not yet a third class petty officer. I had enough time in rate to take the third class petty officer test before I reported for duty. I didn't have the skills yet to test for an electronics technician rating, so in December, I had the opportunity to test for third class electricians mate (EM3) that was an easier test to pass. I wouldn't learn if I had passed the test until I was on active duty and aboard ship. The regular Navy doesn't have a high regard for reservists.

They had some derogatory things to say about us, so I may have had to spend my whole career on mess cook duty.

I was assigned to the USS General W.A. Mann TAP 112 – a personnel attack transport, whose homeport was Seattle, Washington. When I went aboard the ship in January 1957, I didn't know whether I had passed the test for Electricians Mate Third Class (EM3). Soon after reporting aboard ship, I was notified that I did pass the test and was saved from mess cook duty.

The General Mann was a troop transport that sailed from Seattle, Washington to Yokohama, Japan, then on to Inchon, Korea. I made sixteen trips to the Far East in twenty-two months of duty! Some side ventures took us to Taipei, Taiwan, and Guam so I saw a lot of the Far East.

During my navy service, I realized that if I wanted the kind of life I envisioned, I needed to get an education. Early on, I bonded with a fellow electricians mate from Burlington, Wisconsin. We shared similar ideas and ideals and discussed our desired futures. He told me that he was going to Milwaukee School of Engineering (MSOE), a school that was on a quarterly plan year-round and you could get your degree in three years of continuous schooling. While on a thirty-day leave, I visited MSOE in Milwaukee, Wisconsin and was tested and accepted for admission when I got out of the Navy. I requested and received an early discharge in December 1958, so I could start school January 3, 1959. I enrolled in a course of Electronic Communications Technology, a two-year, eight-quarter curriculum leading to an Associate Degree in Applied Science. That was all the time I thought I could afford to spend before starting a family. By doubling up on classes, I completed the curriculum in seven quarters.

In March 1960, I graduated with honors. This was a great accomplishment for me ... a guy who had wandered aimlessly through high school as an average student.

MSOE has an exceptional record of placing their students in industry. At the end of each school year, many corporations came to the school to recruit engineers. I had never interviewed for a job before, so I volunteered to be the student representative for corporate recruiters. I set up the interview appointments for the class and consequently got the pick of times for any and all of the companies that came for student interviews. In this way, I could learn what was expected in a job interview.

One of the corporations that came to our school early was Sandia Corporation in Albuquerque, New Mexico. They were the Research and Development arm of the Atomic Energy Commission so you had to have a security clearance to work there. That clearance took about three months to complete so that was the reason for the early interviews. I made a favorable impression on the recruiter – plus being in the top ten percent of my class, which was a requirement by them – and was invited to travel to Albuquerque for an interview by their engineers. On a cold winter afternoon in February 1960 – it was about thirteen degrees below zero and the ground was covered with snow – I left Milwaukee for New Mexico arriving late at night. The next morning I got up to clear skies and twenty-degree temperatures. By noon, it was fifty degrees and everyone was walking around without a coat on ... a wintertime luxury I had not experienced in my whole life! The interview went well and I was offered a job if I passed the security clearance. The position paid $485/month, a better than average salary in those days and the best salary I had seen coming from the recruiters at school. Their benefits were five weeks vacation a year and the sun shined an average of 350 days a year. We had found paradise! In March, upon graduation, we packed up and headed for Albuquerque for my first job out of school.

Sandia Corporation
Albuquerque, New Mexico

At Sandia, I was assigned to the Component Development Lab. Their charter was to qualify electronic components used in the weapons systems and to design systems electronics for use in hostile environments. The first years at Sandia were spent working on the vacuum tube components used in existing atomic weapons systems. It was staffed with engineers who had designed the first atomic weapons whose circuitry was designed around vacuum tubes. They were there to service the equipment and maintain or update the existing stockpile of weapons. As such, they were in their 50s and 60s and just waiting to retire. These engineers had no interest or the education to work with semiconductors.

To digress a moment…While in school, I supplemented our income by playing in a dance band a few times a month. One of the musicians was a Marquette University student who described to me how a semiconductor worked. It required very little energy, unlike a vacuum tube that had a filament like a light bulb that generated the electrons that caused the flow of electricity. That seemed like a fairy tale to me. It sounded kind of like perpetual motion.

I was very interested after hearing more about them in school. It was so early in the evolution of semiconductors that I took a class from an instructor who had never seen a transistor and was teaching from a book on germanium diodes (an archaic technology that was replaced by a more efficient silicon process).

Semiconductors became commercially available in 1959. First available as transistors (individual devices), the major uses were in military applications and later, in consumer products such as television sets and radios. In 1961 and 1962, Fairchild Semiconductor and Texas Instruments co-invented a process to put multiple transistors and resistors and capacitors on a single chip of silicon called an integrated circuit (IC). In the mid 1960s, Bob Widlar – often called the father of the linear integrated circuit – invented the linear integrated circuit technology that required transistors, resistors, and capacitors to be integrated in/on to a silicon chip.

When Sandia began testing and specifying semiconductors for weapon applications it piqued my interest and I quickly volunteered to work with them since the older engineers didn't want anything to do with the new technology. I took courses at the University of New Mexico at lunchtime and in the evenings that included Semiconductor Theory and the Physics of Semiconductors; how they work, how they are manufactured, and the material they are made of. A more thorough description of Semiconductors is available on the World Wide Web at Wikipedia.org. I also took Boolean algebra classes and learned to use Venn Diagrams to solve digital design logical equations. Circuit designs – using Venn Diagrams – could be minimized using basic logic components; gates, flop-flops, and exclusive OR/AND circuits.

As a research and development (R&D) facility, Sandia had representatives from all the semiconductor companies knocking on their doors and the Sandia engineers had the opportunity to see new products early in their life cycle. In addition to Fairchild and Texas Instruments, there were visits from Signetics, Transitron, Westinghouse, Motorola – all the players in this new industry.

Sandia started buying and testing these products in 1963 and 1964. Most of the testing was done to ensure they could function in extreme temperatures and harsh shock and vibration environments (we called this shake, rattle, and roll testing) as well as in extreme radiation environments. I recall testing some of the first Fairchild silicon planar transistors – the 2N697 – that cost $150 each at the time, and eventually less than twenty-five cents.

There wasn't any test equipment commercially available to test the parameters of the device for radiation tolerance, so we had to design and build that equipment ourselves in the early days of 1964-65. This was another great learning opportunity for me in equipment design.

The results of the tests told us we needed a better semiconductor design than was commercially available. I was able to use my semiconductor theory education to help me manage a development contract with Motorola Semiconductor to design a custom transistor that would withstand higher radiation levels and temperature – what the circuits would experience in an outer space environment during an anti-missile or missile attack. I thoroughly enjoyed the challenge. I had to learn more and more about the design and manufacturing processes. Radiation tolerance specifications was a classified specification, so I could only tell them how to change the process to improve radiation tolerance and not what the parameters should be since it was a classified specification.

As time went on, TI, Motorola, and Fairchild began building integrated circuits. The first circuits were mainly gates and flip-flops in varying technologies: ECL, CTL, RTL, DTL, TTL. Sandia needed more sophisticated equipment to test these ICs that were being produced. Equipment to test device parameters at temperature extremes and the effect of radiation exposure on device performance was not commercially available. Fairchild Test and Instrumentation in California was in the business of providing production line test equipment to semiconductor manufacturers for testing individual transistors. They adapted that tester to test multi-pin ICs. We contracted with them to manufacture a custom designed tester – the Fairchild 4000 IC tester – that was capable of automatically testing the device parameters at temperature and voltage extremes; room temperature, -55ºC (Celsius) and at +125ºC and record the electrical parameters. It was my responsibility to write a proposal for submission to the Atomic Energy Commission for approval and funding.

In 1965, Sandia was given a project to build the logic for an electronic artillery fuse. This circuitry had to fit on a 3½ inch printed circuit (PC) board in the nose of the shell. We designed an integrated circuit version of the discrete device design with gates and flip-flops utilizing the Boolean algebra theory to optimize the component count. During this development, a research division of Westinghouse Electric in Newbury Park, California headed up by Fred Innis came to Sandia looking for a project to test a new process they were developing to build custom integrated circuits using multi-layer interconnections. This would reduce the interconnections of the components and, at the same time, reduce the size of a monolithic chip of silicon. I think – but can't substantiate it – that this was either the first or one of the first designs using multi-layer metal interconnects to be manufactured in the industry. Our device was in development for about eighteen months before they successfully built one working prototype. Westinghouse would not take an order for more because they said the process wasn't ready for mass production. This was the beginning of the next development in semiconductors, large-scale integration (LSI). Today, they have perfected the use of several layers of metal over oxide insulation interconnections to connect the thousands of components needed in the design of a microprocessor device such as used in todays microprocessor designs. Sandia received this test sample about the time I had decided to leave Sandia so I didn't have an opportunity to complete the testing process.

All of these examples are intended to explain how I was fortunate enough to be in the right place at the right time to experience an abundance of new technology being developed almost weekly. Working at an R&D lab exposed the engineers to the latest in development from the many manufacturers in the high technology sector. I had stumbled into this fantastic opportunity because of the desire for a good paying job and a favorable weather environment... a little fate and a lot of planning.

To digress a bit from this line of thought, I was not happy with my progress at Sandia. I thought I should have been given more responsibility and better raises over the years. I set a goal for myself that if I couldn't make a good middle class living wage by the time I was thirty-five, I would leave Sandia. I was working in a research environment that thrives on Ph.Ds. and Masters Degrees for its engineers and I had an associate degree in Electronic Communications. That held me back from further growth at Sandia. I loved what I was doing and the family loved Albuquerque but always living on the edge wasn't what I had planned for my family. Borrowing to buy a new washer, paying doctor bills in installments because we couldn't afford to pay it all at once wasn't the way I wanted to provide for my family. It was time to look for other work. Now the question was where and what. This was a large change in our future. I wanted to be involved in the growing new technology of integrated circuits.

I was offered a sales position with a local semiconductor manufacturers representative, covering the Southwest but I didn't want to be away from home as much as the position required. I also knew that a marketing position would take advantage of my engineering experience and lead to a salary that would meet my goals. Little did I know at the time that this career change would also put me in a position that required being away from home for extended periods of time.

The next decision was location. Motorola, Texas Instruments and Fairchild Semiconductor were candidates. I decided against Motorola because if the job didn't work out, there weren't any other semiconductor companies in the Phoenix area from which to choose if I wanted to change jobs. Texas Instruments worked five nine-hour-days and I had vowed not to work overtime after seeing how hard my dad worked and how little time he spent with the family. I was interested in Fairchild, but the local sales representative wouldn't help me in getting an introduction for an interview. I was looking for my next opportunity but not very hard. There wasn't any urgency, just a desire.

Let me get back to the story. Since I was the one who had written the machine's specification and placed the order for the Fairchild 4000 Integrated Circuit Tester, I made a visit to the Mountain View, California facility in 1965 to check on the manufacturing progress of the machine. One of the engineers in our lab asked me to go over to the Fairchild Semiconductor facility, while I was in California, to negotiate a specification for a specially tested version of a linear operational amplifier circuit called the UA702. I didn't know anything about linear circuits because I was a digital engineer, but he said that wasn't an issue in this case. After my visit with Fairchild Instrumentation, I went over to the semiconductor facility to talk to the linear marketing department about the device specification.

Now here is where either fate or planning came into play. I met with Jack Gifford, the Product Marketing Manager for Linear Circuits to discuss the Sandia specification. When we were through, he invited me out for dinner. He had just been promoted to Linear Integrated Circuit Product Marketing Manager at the headquarters in Mountain View from a sales position in Los Angeles and he and his wife were living in a motel on El Camino Real in Mountain View. He asked if his wife, Rhodean, could join us. During dinner, he asked if I would be interested in coming to work for him. I reiterated that I was a digital engineer and knew nothing about linear circuits. He said he could teach me all I needed to know about linear circuits. I told him my main interest was working with this new semiconductor process called metal oxide silicon (MOS) that I had been following in the *IEEE Spectrum* (the Institute for Electronic and Electrical Engineering magazine) that reported on new technologies and electronic developments. As an aside, Sandia was using a mechanical delay line in one of our applications and a semiconductor shift register could perform that function electronically. Sandia purchased some of the first 25-bit MOS shift registers that were being manufactured by a MOS company called General MicroElectronics, GMe. This was another spin-off from Fairchild. Jack said that the Linear Products division was marketing the only commercially available MOS device being offered by Fairchild. If I would join him, I could be responsible for marketing that product. It was a six channel analog switch being used to download data from space satellites. He offered me a thirty percent raise over my Sandia salary and I was ecstatic. Now all I had to do was convince my wife to move. We both loved the desert. I promised her that we would go to California for five years to make whatever fame and fortune we could and then we would go back to Albuquerque. She agreed, and in 1966 I made the switch from engineering to marketing. Forty-eight years later, we are still in California.

Being in the right place at the right time.

In addition to fate and planning, there is a third effect on life. *Being in the right place at the right time.* The 1960s brought the development of the semiconductor, which fostered the age of computers, calculators, and data storage devices (memory) and the advent of a whole new concept in television, radio, and communications. The computer and memory development was the genesis for the information age in the coming years.

I had the good fortune to be at Fairchild Semiconductor working among the leaders in technology and to participate in the early greatness of the semiconductor revolution. Creativity in Silicon Valley was abundant. The old adage, "necessity is the mother of invention" was prevalent. You can compare these people to what Henry Ford created in the Automobile Age of the 1920s and 1930s. When the demand for cars became greater than the number that could be built by hand, Mr. Ford created the assembly line. The engineers and scientists of the semiconductor age created the manufacturing process for making the mass-produced products that have changed the world.

The Evolution of the Industry

In just over 50 years, we would see the growth of a new industry that has impacted automobiles to space ships, communications from "snail mail" and telephones to email and the Internet, from calculators to personal computers, from file cabinets of records to data storage in the "cloud."

This new industry got a major boost from Dr. William Shockley. Dr. Shockley was working at Bell Laboratory on semiconductor technology in 1947-55. He became unhappy at Bell Labs with management bureaucracy and in 1956, left to form Shockley Semiconductor in Mountain View, California… the beginning of Silicon Valley. He recruited a group of engineers and scientists to work with him on his semiconductor theory. In short order, the same thing happened at Shockley Labs. The team he recruited grew unhappy with his management style and left en masse. Shockley deemed them "The Traitorous 8; Julius Blank, Victor Grinich, Jean Hoerni, Eugene Kliener, Jay Last, Gordon Moore, Robert Noyce, and Sheldon Roberts. This team of engineers and scientists found funding from Sherman Fairchild at Fairchild Camera and Instruments and formed Fairchild Semiconductor in 1957 in Mountain View, California.

Fairchild Semiconductor 1957-

Fairchild became a magnet for creative engineers and scientists and would become the parent company of similar defections over the years. This is not meant to belittle the contributions of other major semiconductor companies but Fairchild fathered a large list of new start-up companies that have been called the "Fairchildren" companies. History books have been written about the "Fairchildren".

These men created the planar process for making transistors and later made mass produced integrated circuits possible. Ultimately, Dr. Noyce and Jack Kilby of Texas Instruments developed a process for putting multiple components on a single slice of silicon at about the same time. After some contentious debate over which one invented the integrated circuit, both were credited with the invention.

In 1964, another innovative circuit designer, Bob Widlar joined Fairchild. He is credited with the invention of the linear integrated circuit; operational amplifiers, voltage regulators, etc. He was eventually unhappy with how he was rewarded for his creativity and made a demand for better compensation and was turned down. In 1966, he and his process-engineering manager, Dave Talbert left Fairchild to join National Semiconductor, an East Coast transistor manufacturer that had fallen on hard times and was bought by Peter Sprague, a member of the Sprague Electric family. He combined it with Molectro, a West Coast company in Santa Clara, California and relocated the main operation there.

Bob Widlar was a brilliant, eccentric engineer who founded a whole new industry with the creation of linear integrated circuit designs. Stories about him are legion. One humorous story during the early years of National comes to mind. National was on a tight budget and one function that was abandoned was the maintenance of the landscaping on the campus. This disturbed Widlar to see the scruffy landscaping. One day, on his way to work from the Santa Cruz Mountains in his Mercedes-Benz convertible he brought a sheep from a meadow and staked it on the corporate lawn to "mow" the grass. This was chronicled in the *San Jose Mercury News*.

Fairchild also became an attraction for some of the best marketing and sales personnel in the industry. Floyd Kvamme, Don Valentine, Jerry Sanders, Tom Bay and Jack Gifford among many others were in marketing and sales at Fairchild during this era. These people were mentors that provided invaluable training for my new career and were people that had a major impact on the industry, as we know it today. All would subsequently go off to start other companies.

Fairchild and the evolution of the semiconductor industry

I joined Fairchild Semiconductor Linear Marketing in March of 1966. I accepted a position in linear marketing, but my end goal was to be a part of the MOS technology development. I learned a lot about marketing and sales from Jack Gifford and will be forever grateful for his tutelage. Success in business will often be as the result of finding the right mentor to guide you along the learning path.

In September of 1966 two more engineers joined our group who would play an important role in my future – A. C. "Mike" Markkula and Mike Scott.

From 1959 to 1968, the predominant technology for manufacturing integrated circuits used a bipolar semiconductor process. It was the next step in the electronic evolution that reduced power consumption and increased component density from the first generation of electronics that used vacuum tubes. The next new technology was the metal oxide semiconductor (MOS) process that allowed for a much higher density of components on a single chip of silicon with much lower power dissipation. The first commercially available MOS integrated circuits contained about 100 – 150 individual components. In 2015, the fifth generation of the microprocessor contains 1.3 billion transistors on a single chip! Developments in processing equipment technology and accuracy allowed chip sizes to increase from about 0.1 inch on a side to over 0.5 inch today. In 1965, these devices were photo-etched on a wafer of silicon that was about one inch in diameter and about one hundredth of an inch thick. In 2015, a wafer of silicon is dinner plate size – over 12 inches in diameter. The vast majority of all semiconductor components today are manufactured using some form of MOS technology.

MOS was still in its infancy and a majority of the work was being done at Fairchild Research and Development Labs in Palo Alto, California. Before a process can be manufactured commercially, it is necessary to develop a repeatable process that does not require skilled engineers, just skilled technicians, to operate. Without a repeatable process in the manufacturing department, there wasn't a need or position within Fairchild for a MOS marketing manager. I got involved with any and all marketing functions done in this area along with my duties in linear marketing. I *assumed* the marketing leadership role in hopes of one day being promoted to fill that position. The primary team of R&D engineers that I interfaced with included Bob Noyce, head of R&D and later the President of Fairchild Semiconductor, Gordon Moore, Andrew Grove, Les Vadasz and Frank Wanlass. I spent a considerable amount of time learning the ins and outs of the process and philosophy from these engineers at Fairchild R&D.

In 1968, MOS technology became a viable technology and a new industry was born. Fairchild moved the process out of R&D and created a process-engineering department within the manufacturing division to develop both standard components and custom designed products to a customer's specifications. These engineers created custom LSI circuits in both bipolar and MOS technologies. I was transferred into this new marketing department for bipolar memory and MOS components as a Product Marketing Engineer working for Jerry Larkin.

As all of this growth of new technologies began to emerge, I assumed the "factory marketing voice" of Fairchild MOS to our customers. I traveled around the country giving seminars on the virtues of this new technology and how it would change semiconductor development. Giving seminars on this new technology was a job that I thoroughly enjoyed. It helped me get more self-assurance and a better understanding of how it would be utilized as well. You must believe in yourself to have the confidence that you can do your job effectively.

While I was at Hughes Aircraft to give a seminar to their design engineering department on the MOS technology and the types of products Fairchild was developing, a loud engineer in a room of about thirty or forty people asked me what my function was at Fairchild. I told him I was a product marketing engineer. He loudly told everyone that he wasn't going to waste his time listening to a "sales guy." I told him that I would like to tell my story and if, at any time, he thought I was wasting his time, just raise his hand and I would stop my presentation and leave. At the end of about an hour presentation, that same engineer asked me if I would repeat the presentation to a group of division managers. This was a real confidence builder for me and another lesson in personal development.

The question of what to build led to a department managed by Bob Schreiner to solicit custom built designs. The key engineers most notably were James Downey, Bob Ulricksen, Dan Floyd, and Rob Walker.

In the process of marketing in this development group, I coined and trademarked the phrase MOS Array Integrated Circuit (MOSAIC) and began creating brochures and presentations to market our capabilities.

A bipolar group within the custom array design department used Micro MATRIX for their marketing presentations.

As additional products came within the capability of these new system concepts, a "standard products" department was established. Lee Boysel – an IBM computer systems engineer – joined Fairchild as a design-engineering manager. His expertise was in designing computer architecture circuitry. He recruited a crack team of engineers that began building LSI component parts that were equivalent, at the time, to a full printed circuit board of bipolar circuits. The first standard LSI part to be designed was a 64 bit by 8 bit read-only memory (ROM) using "four phase clock systems" for system timing and control. The device was pushing the capabilities of the processing technology at that time, being almost a quarter of an inch on each side. The ROM was the beginning of a whole new era of computer hardware structure. Today they build ROMs, programmable ROMs (PROM), electrically programmable ROMs (ePROM), and field programmable gate arrays (FPGA) in mega-bit device sizes compared to the first 256-bit ROM of the late 1960s.

The Boysel design team developed a "bit slice" approach to building the central processing unit (CPU) of a computer. The device was a "vertical" 4-bit slice of the CPU that could be connected together to form different sized CPUs. For example, two slices would make an 8-bit microprocessor. Four slices would make a 16-bit microprocessor and so on. The CPU used the four-phase clock system to control the operation.

Another creative design by the Boysel team was a 16-bit analog to digital converter for the General Electric Military division in Schenectady, New York.

... And the exodus began!

Boysel's team tried to sell the concept of building a bit-slice microprocessor to Dr. Noyce, then the president of Fairchild, which met with little enthusiasm. He would later leave Fairchild in 1968, taking the key design engineers with him to found Four Phase Systems – another start-up – to build computer systems utilizing similar MOS designs. The company subsequently built and manufactured one of the first computer systems to use MOS technology. The first big order was for the Sabre system used for airline reservations. Incidentally, I was devastated that I didn't get invited to go with them.

Shortly thereafter, the Dr. Noyce group of engineers and scientists left Fairchild in 1968 and started Intel Corporation to build MOS memory devices. Their vision for the future was a 1024-bit dynamic random access memory device (DRAM), another market that was visionary in nature at that time. Their work on the MOS process perfected a new version of MOS called Silicon Gate Technology.

The clocking system for four-phase logic design was difficult to control. The MOS process was refined at Intel to include Silicon Gate Technology (SGT). While at Fairchild in 1963, Frank Wanlas patented another form of MOS technology – Complimentary Metal Oxide Semiconductor (CMOS). It was further developed to create a better design medium for many new applications. First as low power logic circuits, replicating bipolar designed Gates, and Flip Flops and then complex LSI devices followed quickly.

All of this interest in MOS technology finally opened a position for a MOS Product Marketing Manager and I thought I was wired for that position. Lo and behold, someone higher up wanted his field sales protégé to have a position in corporate marketing and he was given the job! Needless to say, I was crushed again. I guess all things happen for a reason.

In 1967, a group of operations and marketing management people left Fairchild to join Widlar and Talbot at National Semiconductor when it moved from Danbury, Connecticut to Santa Clara, California. Charles Sporck became CEO and Fred Bialek, Pierre Lamond, and C.E. Pausa set up the operations side of the business. Don Valentine and Floyd Kvamme were the marketing department. Don would later become one of the early venture capitalists (VCs) in the valley. At the time, their predominant products were linear circuits created by the brilliant engineering team of Widlar and Talbot.

In addition to the linear circuits process, the new management team recruited Ken Moyle from Hewlett-Packard (HP), an MOS process engineer and Dan Izumi an MOS design engineer. They began designing memory components and calculator chips for the burgeoning calculator market in Japan. The recruitment of Jeff Kalb followed from Texas Instruments to second source the Series 51/71 TTL bipolar logic line of digital integrated circuits. From a resurrected transistor company, they created a competitive integrated circuit semiconductor company.

I was still chafing from being passed over for the position of MOS product marketing manager I coveted at Fairchild. Of all the spin-offs from Fairchild Semiconductor, I felt my best chance and best fit was with the people I knew at National Semiconductor. I heard that they were recruiting an MOS marketing manager, so I applied for the position. It helped that Don Valentine, the Director of Marketing and Floyd Kvamme, the Product Marketing Manager knew me from their time at Fairchild. I was offered, and accepted the position.

They interviewed Barry Cash from Texas Instruments and he would later join MOS Technology, a TI spin-off for MOS development.

In 1969, Jerry Sanders and Jack Gifford left Fairchild and founded Advanced Micro Devices. After a falling out, Jack left AMD and founded Maxim Integrated Circuits yet another successful linear semiconductor company.

In 1973, the Schreiner team left Fairchild to form another company: Synertek, Inc. to build standard products as well as custom designs... another spin-off of brainpower and technology.

In 1981, Bob Dobkin – a protégé of Bob Widlar's – and Bob Swanson the manufacturing manager for linear circuits left National Semiconductor to found Linear Technology. All of these companies became major players in the linear integrated circuit (LIC) industry and continue to be major players today.

These were heady times to be involved with this new technological advancement in semiconductor processing. Fairchild was the place to be in the late 1950s and 1960s. These spin-offs began to dissipate their position in the industry and Texas Instruments and Motorola became more formidable competitors.

National Semiconductor March 1969

In March 1969, I resigned from Fairchild Semiconductor and joined National Semiconductor as the product-marketing manager for MOS products. National would grow, during my time there, from $7 million in 1969 to $700 million by 1977. This is a tremendous growth rate for any company and it was very exciting to be a part of that growth.

The MOS product line was just beginning to flourish. It was a very busy time and the phone never stopped ringing. I developed a disdain for telephones that exists today. The product line consisted primarily of memory devices. The first such devices were shift registers to replace mechanical delay line memories, and random access memory to replace core memory. All in all, it was a very fast moving time in semiconductor memory growth to replace the old electro-mechanical devices that were large and power consuming. Recall that Intel Corporation was founded to build random access memory devices exclusively.

Calculator chip development

In the 1960s, a business calculator was an electro-mechanical device that cost as much as the personal computers of today, $500 to $2,000. In 1969 Brother, a sewing machine manufacturer in Japan, and Busicomp, a Japanese calculator company contracted with National to design a chipset to build an electronic business calculator. This endeavor was a significant part in semiconductor calculator history. As hard as they tried, National engineers could not get the four devices to work together properly for technical reasons. After a couple of years trying without success, Busicomp contacted Intel to see if they could do something for them. Ted Hoff, a young Intel engineer came up with the idea of building a four-bit microprocessor on a chip that could be programmed to operate as a calculator. It became known as the Intel 4004 microprocessor. National subsequently lost the contract… and a position in history.

In 1971, the 4004 and Ted Hoff were credited with creating the beginning of the microprocessor age. This 4-bit microprocessor is the genesis of today's microprocessor chips. It has progressed through a series of continual upgrades to the latest rendition of the Intel microprocessor reported to be a processor with forty-eight processing units, called cores, on a chip. Such a device will be able to do forty-eight functions simultaneously. Now the challenge is to develop the software that will make use of this computing power.

MITS

Ed Roberts, an Air Force tech that had been based at Kirkland Air Force Base in Albuquerque, New Mexico started a company, Military Instrumentation Technical Support (MITS), to service military electronics on the base. He began to branch out into the new world of semiconductor electronics and set up shop in a two-bedroom house on San Mateo Avenue. They used the same National chipset for their design. The combination of technical difficulties, slow delivery of the chipsets by National, and the lack of appropriate funding by MITS resulted in cancellation of the project.

Meeting Bill Gates and Paul Allen the first time.

MITS continued to work in the new field of integrated circuit system design and later announced the Altair 8800, an early entrant into the personal computer world. The Altair was introduced as a kit computer in *Popular Electronics* magazine with great interest among the computer techies of the era.

During a visit to MITS on one occasion, Ed Roberts wanted to introduce me to his software design team. They were two young college dropouts intensely working in a back bedroom. The room was full of cables – hanging over the curtain rods and laying across the floor – connected to printers and computer terminals. They were busy designing the operating system for the Altair. We went back to the bedroom and he introduced me to Bill Gates and Paul Allen. They took a quick moment to be introduced and continued coding. Little did I know that I would meet Bill Gates years later under totally different circumstances? Ed Roberts eventually went back to school and became a medical doctor and practiced in Georgia.

My Promotion to Director of Marketing

In 1972, Floyd Kvamme was promoted to VP of Operations, and I succeeded him as director of marketing. This position included the management of the division product marketing managers, providing technical support to the advertising agency on the advertising content for new product introductions, and directing the training of the Field Applications Engineers (FAE).

On a quarterly basis I would go to Los Angeles to meet with the Chiat/Day Advertising Agency copywriters and agency principles to talk about upcoming product introductions. These were exciting times listening to the copywriters come up with ideas for new product ads. It was so exciting to listen to the advertising banter. As I got caught up in the planning, I would suggest a headline for a product and Jay Chiat would say, "Suggesting a headline will guarantee it doesn't get used." (Chiat/Day was the advertising agency that created the 1984 Super Bowl ad for the announcement of the Macintosh computer for Apple Computer. It has been the top rated ad of all Super Bowl advertisements and still is today, thirty years later!)

The creation of Field Application Engineers to support our sales engineers and customers in designing in our proprietary circuits was a National innovation and it became a standard in the industry. The technical support of system designs utilizing the ever-increasing complexity of medium scale (MSI) and large-scale integrated (LSI) circuits made them a necessity.

In this capacity, I had a close relationship with National Semiconductor's Applications Engineering Manager Dale Mrazek. Dale was one of the best digital design and application engineers I have ever seen. He personified the saying, "Necessity is the mother of invention." He specialized in communications engineering and identified a "need" in the emerging computer industry. This need resulted in the development of Tri-State Logic™.

Tri-State Logic, the design and process, was patented (patent number 41,94,132 dated 5/30/78) and the name Tri-State Logic was trademarked.

National announced this new concept in bipolar design by giving seminars around the world on the concept. A competing semiconductor company followed our presenters around the country telling the design engineers that Tri-State Logic wouldn't work and could potentially burn up their system. Finally, a few years later, they copied the concept and announced the invention of Three State Logic. Note that they could not use the Tri-State Logic name because National Semiconductor had already trademarked it.

Working with Dale created one of my most exciting marketing coups. I was going to make a sales call on Digital Equipment Corporation (DEC) and Data General in the Boston area regarding a National MOS keyboard encoder they were using. Dale knew that his new circuit design was needed by someone at DEC but didn't know which engineer. He gave me the specification for the DM 8094 and asked me to find out who needed it and explain to them how it solved their problem. When we were through with the keyboard encoder discussion, I asked the engineer what other problems he had that we may be able to solve for him. He described a need on the bus structure of the PDP-11 and why it was a computer problem. Again, *fate* stepped in. I said, "You are the engineer I am looking for." I showed him the product and how it worked and he became very excited and called the purchasing agent to order 100,000 of them without even knowing the cost or the part number. On paper, that doesn't sound very exciting, but I was ecstatic! To be able to be a part of the leading edge of another engineering breakthrough with a new product is very exciting for a marketing or sales engineer. Dale eventually designed a series of parts he could use to build the DEC PDP-8 computer on one small 8" x 12" card instead of two 16"x16" cards. Thus began another evolution in computer design.

A New Innovation - An Inexpensive Calculator

First a little background. Each year, a company has to develop a business plan for the coming year. It was the responsibility of the marketing department of each product line to forecast those sales by part type and price by quarter. In the 1970s it was done by hand with pencil and paper and a calculator. This was a grueling manual exercise. Today it is done with a spreadsheet program that does the calculating. It was my job to assimilate all of the information from five marketing managers and put it into the company business plan. This was done on a big piece of butcher paper. The so-called consumer calculators sold for more than $100 at that time. The Commodore calculator I owned used an odd sized battery and I was forever trying to find a store that sold them. The battery would invariably die late at night during planning season and these calculators were not rechargeable nor did they work on electricity like today's designs. This precipitated another "necessity is the mother of invention" moment.

During that time, 1972 and 1973, an engineer in the digital design group said he had an idea for how to design a calculator on a chip – it had never been done before – and asked what features I would like to see in a consumer calculator. My dream calculator would be an eight-digit floating-point calculator – to display tens of millions of dollars – that used a 9-volt battery – easy to find at any store – and sell for under $40, affordable for every home. At this time, MOS technology would not operate on 9 volts but after some months of engineering they figured out how to make that happen by designing a voltage doubler on the chip. The next hurdle was the price. The light-emitting diode (LED) displays were too expensive to use in a $40 calculator. LEDs cost $1.25 per digit. A floating-point calculator chip took up 25 percent more semiconductor circuit area than a fixed-point design, and the cost of a keyboard and case would drive the manufacturing cost well above that, which would allow a profit from a $40 selling price.

We settled on a 6-digit display with a fixed-point calculator chip technology that could meet the design cost. In other words, the decimal point was fixed on the display so you could display up to $9,999.99, or drop the fixed decimal point on the display and add up to $999,999. My thought was that the market for an inexpensive hand held calculator was the housewife who would take it to the store to figure out how much something cost and to stay on a budget… probably not the right reason, but the right idea for an inexpensive calculator. Thus, the first low cost calculator was born. A lot of people take credit for this calculator and for being first to market. This was my first lesson in an old adage, "Success has many owners but a failure has none." Texas Instruments takes credit for being the first to have a low cost machine, but it was the National 6 digit entry that forced them to reduce their prices to compete.

It was not a popular device for the manufacturing manager, because of its complexity. He came to me saying that I was "killing the profit of his production line" with these kinds of design requirements. He urged the president, Charlie Sporck, to drop the program. I made my pitch to him by telling him I would quit my job, take responsibility for selling the device as a sales rep for no salary but a 10 percent commission for every part sold. His response was, "You better-ass be right. Now get back to work." The program went on and I kept my job.

It became so successful that National created a consumer company called Novus that manufactured and sold the complete calculator. Within two years, bank and credit card companies were giving them away as an advertising promotion and they were being sold for under $5. Companies like Texas Instruments and Commodore and a number of Japanese manufacturers were big players in this market and it became a very competitive market.

National Semiconductor - the microprocessor evolution.

The late 1960s and early 1970s were a very fast moving time for calculator and microprocessor development. The Intel 4004 started a move toward building microprocessors. From 1971 to 1974, the major semiconductor companies, National, Motorola, Intel, Zilog, MOS Technology, Signetics, Fairchild and others were designing and building 8-bit microprocessors. In 1973, National announced the first 16-bit integrated microprocessor, the IMP-16. This was, by microprocessor standards, an elegant design. It consisted of four 4-bit slices of a CPU connected together to make the machine. It became the target of the 8-bit competitors who claimed that it took twice as much memory to program a 16-bit machine compared to an 8-bit machine and would therefore cost more – all of which was not true. The efficiencies of a double byte (8 bits = one byte) instruction word requires less memory and provides a faster execution speed.

In the early 1970s, a group of managers from Certified Grocers, a cooperative of independent super markets with a conceptual system specification, was brought up to Santa Clara by Tom Anthony, the Regional Sales Manager for Southern California. They wanted to develop a point-of-sale (POS) system for supermarket checkout. The system included barcode scanners, inventory management, price checking, and other applications needed to streamline the supermarket computer system. I realized that it was beyond my capabilities to comprehend and brought in some of the microprocessor designers to discuss their needs. The result was that National got involved in the manufacture and the distribution of these systems and formed National Advanced Systems, a division that built and maintained these systems. The division was sold in 1987 to ICL.

In 1974, National announced a single chip 16-bit microprocessor whose acronym was PACE, Processing and Control Element. They also announced a competitor to the 8-bit microprocessor revolution called the SC/MP – Simple Cheap Micro Processor – dressed up to be called the Simple Cost-effective Micro Processor.

So you see that in just three short years, the microprocessor revolution *and* the refinement of the metal oxide semiconductor technology was formed. There were so many new designs and applications for microprocessors that they are to numerous to name.

The economy changed and so did my life.

In 1973, the country was in a major recession. 25,000 Lockheed engineers were laid off in Silicon Valley and far more across the country lost their jobs. In 1975, National decided to change their cost centers by creating product divisions that were responsible for all aspects of their business. The position of director of marketing was eliminated. I was given a choice of which marketing position I wanted and I chose the microprocessor division. This started another stage in my life.

The IMP-16 created a lot of interest for its capability. The PACE and SC/MP provided a new opportunity to learn more about microprocessors and their applications in industrial equipment designs. One of the early design-ins was at Sun Electric, an automobile test and instrumentation company in the Chicago area. They were an old-line company that used D'Arsonval meters as measuring devices. Sun wanted to upgrade their test stations to the twentieth century and the IMP-16 was selected for the project.

Unfortunately our manufacturing process not very reliable and we had a lot of false starts. As marketing manager, I had the responsibility of interfacing with unhappy customers on a regular basis. After three years working in a hostile environment and for a manager that I didn't connect with, I began looking for another opportunity. I thought the world of Charlie Sporck and wanted to stay with National so I began looking for an opportunity there first.

That opportunity came in the form of a young engineer, Steve Leininger. He had designed a computer for industrial applications using the SC/MP microprocessor. He also created a programming language compatible with applications in industrial process control. This software was named National Industrial Basic Language (NIBL). They were the building blocks for a customizable system for varying industrial applications. The components were put on 4-inch by 4-inch PC boards that plugged into an industry standard card cage.

A group of us thought there was a substantial market opportunity for this kind of machine. Steve, Phil Roybal, a product marketing manager in the microprocessor division, and I developed a business plan that defined a separate division within National to design, manufacture and sell this industrial computer concept. There were other system divisions at National and we presented our plan to the executive staff of National in hopes of getting funding to set up a new small computer division. The executive staff decided that there wasn't any market for "small computers" and proclaimed that the market was for 370/158s – large mainframe computers – and DEC-11 minicomputers.

As a result, I resigned from National in early 1977 after being with them for 8 years. They had been very good to me, but it was time to move on under the circumstances.

Steve Leininger left National shortly thereafter and went to Fort Worth, Texas to work for Radio Shack. He was the designer of the TRS-80, a highly popular personal computer sold by Radio Shack.

Thirty years later, Charlie Sporck commented to me that he had missed the small computer market.

National had been one of the first companies to give their employees the opportunity to share in the growth of a company by giving them stock options as part of their compensation. These options matured over a four-year period, which was an incentive to keep key people from leaving. National had been quite successful and I had received additional stock options as bonuses throughout my employment. The stock had appreciated by a large percentage over the years and I thought there was enough money in these options to live on for the rest of my family's life so I retired.

This was a big mistake. Within three months, I was bored silly! I was not interested in working the stock market and managing a stock portfolio. I got so lethargic that I was getting up late, reading the paper over breakfast, pulling a few weeds in the yard and then sitting by the pool. This was against my values and lifestyle. I have always believed that time was a terrible thing to waste. At forty-three, I had over half my life yet to live and decided that this was not the way I wanted to live it. I was motivated to find a new endeavor.

Entering the Next Phase of My Life

Hewlett Packard is a large, well-respected company that was building scientific calculators – rather sophisticated devices for this period in the electronic evolution. I felt that our product was compatible with this kind of design and manufacturing technique. In early 1977, I tried to arrange a meeting with the engineering manager at Hewlett Packard to talk about my business plan and vision for small computers. Apparently I didn't have name recognition because I could never get him to return my calls.

In April of 1977, I decided to see if I could get financing from investors to start a company based upon the business plan we had developed for our presentation to the National Semiconductor Executive Staff. There were several venture capital funds in Silicon Valley. Venture capitalists were private equity companies that were formed to invest the funds of their clients in start-up companies. They took a position in the company and received stock in return for the money they invested instead of loaning money to them and charging interest like a bank or lending institution would do.

Don Valentine had been the director of marketing at Fairchild Semiconductor when I was there and was one of the executives that left Fairchild and later joined National Semiconductor. Recall that he was the Director of Marketing at National and the one who hired me when I decided to leave Fairchild. Don left National to form one of the early venture capital funds in Silicon Valley, Sequoia Capital. I knew him and respected him as a businessman, so in early 1977 I took our plan to him in hopes of interesting him in our concept and to encourage him to invest in our business.

After listening to my company presentation he asked me what I wanted to do. I told him I saw an opportunity for small computers and I wanted to be a part of that industry. It was a new concept in computing technology and I thought it would be a great selling challenge to sell it into such a new marketplace. He asked if I knew what my old Fairchild office mates were doing at Apple Computer. I didn't. Those old office mates were Mike Markkula and Mike Scott. You may recall that I said that the two Mikes and I shared a cubicle while working for Jack Gifford at Fairchild Semiconductor.

Again, fate stepped in. Don told me that two scruffy looking kids in sandals with torn Levis and long hair had come to him in November of 1976 asking him for funding to form a company to build their computer.

The Creation of Apple
Computer; The Company

This was the beginning of my trip through the most exciting time of my business life.

Those two kids Don Valentine referred to were the inventors of the Apple II. That would be Steve Jobs and Steve Wozniak. The computer they were showing was the Apple I that "Woz" had designed to show off his design skills to the Homebrew Computer Club, which met at the Stanford Linear Accelerator (SLAC) once a month. He had been giving out the schematic along with a parts list that people could use to build their own computer. Steve Jobs was the entrepreneur that recognized a potential opportunity to make something of this idea and wanted to take it a step farther by building the whole computer in a box instead of just the PC board sans peripherals.

Don, being a proper Easterner, didn't take to hippy kids (ages 21 and 26) who wore sandals and torn Levis and tee shirts but was fascinated by their idea. Venture capitalists usually have a stable of bright consultants that they can contact for an expert opinion on a concept before investing in it. He called Mike Markkula, a Fairchild alumnus and an early member of Intel management, who had left in his early thirties after being passed over for the Marketing Manager position. Don said he asked Mike to go over and check out these two kids and to see if there was any value in their idea. He told me that Mike Markkula never came back and perhaps there was something there that better fit what I had in mind.

Mike Markkula visited the two Steve's (who we called Jobs and Woz for identity purposes) at Don Valentine's behest and recognized a great opportunity when he saw their concept, so he funded the project himself. Mike was financially secure and also had a Masters in Electrical Engineering from UCLA, so was technically competent to grasp the concept they were proposing. The three of them worked out a mutually agreeable deal. Mike would provide working capital and guarantee a line of credit at the Bank of America and they would split the company three ways.

Thus began Apple Computer, Incorporated. Employee numbers 1,2, and 3 were defined. Shortly thereafter, Mike hired Mike ("Scottie") Scott as President of Apple Computer. However, when employee numbers were assigned to accommodate the Bank of America's payroll system, Scottie assigned Steve Wosniak employee number one, Mike Markkula, number two and Steve Jobs, number three. Steve Jobs wanted to be employee number one, so that didn't sit well with him. He had his badge number changed to employee number 0. To my knowledge, there is no number 3 today. Also, Scottie was assigned number 5 but he wanted to be "007" and changed his badge from 5 to 7, so there is also no number 5.

In April of 1977, the first West Coast Computer Show was introduced in San Francisco. It was one of the first conventions of computer geeks in the country. Numerous start-up companies building small computers and peripherals were displaying their expertise.

I went to see what was being shown. The feature spot and the highlight of the show was the Apple Computer booth that was showing a new Apple design called the Apple II. The machine was in a typewriter-like, formed plastic case and used a television as a monitor. The display was in color, a new innovation in computers and showed forty characters on a line, a half page of information on a traditional computer monitor! The demonstration was spectacular and was the hit of the show. The other computers were traditional computer displays showing forty or eighty character black and white images on a computer monitor. What I saw was incredible. I got excited!

After that show, I visited the Apple office in Cupertino, California to see the two Mikes and their operation. They gave me a tour of the company, which consisted of a 20 foot by 60 foot office space on Stevens Creek Boulevard. The entire Apple team was housed there.

Mike Markkula and I talked about my interest and what I wanted to do at Apple. He said they already had two marketing guys, he and Scottie, and didn't need another. I told him that I wanted to *sell* computers. After six years in engineering and twelve years in marketing, I wanted to do something different. Mike said he would consider it but at the time, they didn't have any product to sell and wouldn't have a finished computer for several months.

I went home and put together a proposal that I presented to him a few days later. I said I wanted to be a part of this company and wanted a percentage of the stock and the title of sales vice president. He said that I was asking for more than the president got and he wouldn't pay that much for a salesman. He made me a counter offer on company stock and would make me sales manager, not sales vice president. I said no deal, so he threw my letter in the wastebasket and I went home. After having lunch, I realized I *really* wanted to do this. I went back to Mike, pulled the letter out of the trash, and said, "You got a deal." He said they couldn't put me on the payroll until they started shipping product. They had orders but no product. I wanted to be sure that someone else didn't get MY job, so I worked May, June, and July for nothing. I showed up every day, learned the intricacies of the Apple II, and did circuit testing, loaded program cassettes, worked on sales literature and anything else that needed to be done in a start-up company. Apple shipped fifty machines at the end of July, and on August 6, 1977 I became the fourteenth Apple employee. My salary was $30,000 a year and a percentage of the corporate stock. It would be over three years before I got my wish to be Sales Vice President. I know now that the title really didn't matter. It was the job function that mattered.

Again, there is nothing like being in the right place at the right time. During my twelve years in a marketing capacity, I had learned the trade by being associated with some of the best sales and marketing management talent to exist in the semiconductor industry. As marketing engineers, we had to take the same classes and learn the same basics as the sales engineers – the selling process, marketing literature development, product presentations, advertising strategies, account management – all the functions that supported the marketing and sales of a companies product line. It was all part of the process so it wasn't as if I had no knowledge of sales, it was that I had never been a "bag carrying" salesman. I was a student of the art of marketing and sales and wanted the opportunity to use this training. Mike Markkula gave me that opportunity – to be a salesman without any previous experience. I will be forever grateful for his confidence in me. Most companies would not even consider hiring a sales person to run their sales department with no previous experience.

Networking and professional association in the high tech world has its advantages. The three of us – Mike Markkula, Mike Scott, and I had a great working relationship over the years. As I mentioned previously, our relationship goes back to 1966 at Fairchild Semiconductor. Later, when I was director of marketing for National Semiconductor, I recruited Mike Scott to join me as the hybrid circuits product marketing manager. He held this position for several years but had stated when I hired him that he wanted to get into manufacturing. When the hybrid-manufacturing manager left, Mike and I campaigned successfully for him to take that position. He had a degree in Nuclear Physics from USC *and* a photographic memory, so was more than capable.

Back to the story.

The Corporate Vision

We each had a vision for Apple Computer as a personal computer company. These visions were synergistic and focused. The fact that the two Mikes and I were long term colleagues allowed us to debate topics that were sometimes contentious without fear of retribution as often happens in corporate politics. We held a common vision for the development of the personal computer industry and how to best execute that vision within our area of responsibility. This helped to make a successful company management team. I have often been asked if we knew it was going to be as successful as it turned out to be. We had no idea how large an opportunity this would become, but none of us ever considered the possibility of failure.

Mike Markkula had experience in marketing at Fairchild Semiconductor and Intel. As chairman of the board and marketing vice president, he had a vision for establishing Apple Computer as a leading manufacturer of personal computers.

Mike Scott as president and the first operations manager had a vision for a highly automated manufacturing facility that would provide high quality products at a low cost.

I had a vision for the development of a sales organization that would execute the corporate marketing plan. Creating that team was an exciting challenge for me. Above all, I was involved with the small computers I had envisioned when I left National Semiconductor.

Lest you wonder what happened to the two Steves, I don't mean to diminish their roles in the development, but there have been books written on both Steves and their roles, so I am telling you the "behind the scenes" stories of Apple Computer. There are many, many stories behind the scenes that are instrumental in the development of a company or product that are never told.

Woz was the genius engineer that made it happen. He personified "necessity is the mother of invention." He wanted no part of management. He wanted to be the "engineer" – and was he that!

Jobs had the Personal Computer vision and knew what he wanted Apple to be. He was a perfectionist and was very involved in all aspects of engineering, manufacturing, quality control, and packaging. His focus on perfection made him almost unbearable at times.

This perfection and his vision of a computer on every desk drove the development of the Apple II and the Macintosh later in his career. His vision for new products was a salesman's dream. Getting new products to sell on a regular basis keeps the challenge fresh and exciting. Despite his idiosyncrasies, he was an incredible visionary of new electronic gadgets. If

41

you are interested in knowing more about him, I highly recommend his biography, *Steve Jobs,* written by Walter Isaacson. Steve Wozniak's book *iWoz* is a good reference of Woz's genius.

Jobs was involved in almost everything involving creativity at Apple. The case design was of his choosing. The design of the Apple logo required his blessing. Any new designs had to have his blessing before the engineers could continue their development. His quest for perfection was evident even then. That attribute still existed in 2011 and accounts for much of the Apple product mystique in iPhones, iPods, iPads and in the design of the Apple Stores.

The dichotomy of Steve Jobs

Steve Jobs was a perfectionist with a vision for changing the world through digital technology. The first objective of his vision was to develop an affordable personal computer that would sit on everyone's desktop. The perfectionist in him was in every detail of that vision. What followed has been written about in a number of different ways. What I want to write about is that dichotomy that is Steve Jobs.

Many people have written about his many quirks of perfectionism and attention to detail: the *right* color for a computer, the *right* shape for the iPod, the *right* glass for the iPhone, the *right* color and type of stone for the Apple store flooring, to name just a few.

I recall an incident with our first logo – an Apple logo with six colored stripes. Apple was preparing to make their first shipments of computers in July 1977. We planned on including this 4-inch Apple logo in the shipment for people to display on their car or home window to signify they had bought an Apple Computer. This was an inexpensive form of advertising like an auto dealers license plate frame. When they came in, the printer had not done a good job of registering the colors and there was an overlap between the color stripes. This caused a thin black line that was not ideal. Steve went ballistic and refused the shipment demanding that they redo the order immediately. Most people would have accepted the small anomaly, but not Steve.

The dichotomy is how he lived as a young man. I recall one instance when Steve and I were traveling to Cleveland for a meeting with some dealers. My wife Pat took us to the airport to catch the flight to Cleveland. On the way, he was talking with Pat about revelations he had observed since moving out of his family home. He told her he was amazed, for example, to find out that if he wanted to brush his teeth he had to buy toothpaste. It had always been there for him before.

On another occasion, he was on the way to the airport and his old car, a Volvo as I recall, broke down on the off-ramp overpass to the airport. Someone stopped to help and he said he had to catch a plane and didn't have time to arrange for the car to be towed and if they would do that, he would give them the car and away he went. Not a normal action of most people.

His bathing habits have often been written about. They also showed his lack of detail in his personal life.

His uniform was Levis and black mock turtleneck tee shirt and, in the early days, sandals. Probably the reasoning behind it was so that he didn't have to be concerned about what to wear day-to-day. This was embodied in the statement on the first Apple brochure, "*simplicity is the ultimate sophistication.*"

Like most innovators, Steve did not set out to become wealthy. He set out to change the way people worked and lived through digital technology.

He felt that computers should be made available to all who wanted one. As a visionary, Steve was a marketing and sales person's dream. The most difficult part of creating the next big innovation or the next generation of products is to know what the customer wants or will buy before they do. His vision was so incredibly right-on. While he had disdain for sales and marketing, he was the ultimate sales and marketing person. He often said that the only reason someone becomes a salesman is because they are too dumb to do anything else. Little did he realize that his P.T. Barnum product announcements were, in fact, a selling event that created customer desire to buy the new product he was announcing, every salesman's objective.

Because of the complexity of his personality, you will not find agreement of opinions. He was driven by his vision and was ruthless in his method for achieving the perfection of it. If you contributed to his vision, you were a friend. If you did not contribute, you were a Bozo. If you were peripheral to his vision you were ignored. If you did something to irritate him, you were fired. In any case, his vision was a happening that was exciting to be a part of. It attracted the best of the best in all areas of endeavor at Apple. He was the leader and visionary, but the people behind the product designs were the innovators that created the products that fulfilled his vision.

Steve Wozniak does not get enough credit for his engineering creativity that helped create what Apple Computer, Inc. has become. Woz was the ultimate nerd engineer. He didn't want to be management. He wanted to be recognized as a great engineer. As the architect of the Apple I and the Apple II, his vision was his ability to quantify a computer design efficiently and to solve most engineering problems that arose in the development of the ultimate machine that combined software and hardware. I recall one time he lost all track of time and when he realized that he was very tired, found that he had worked over twenty-four hours without stopping.

Rod Holt joined Apple as the chief engineer to manage the engineering department. He had great credentials in electronic design. He designed a switching regulated power supply that was subsequently patented and became the power supply for the Apple II. Since there was no transformer it was very light, giving the machine a friendly feel.

Rod was a character in his own right, such as being a part of the Kent State riots in 1970 and a social activist. He had two pair of shoes, his everyday hiking boots, and for more formal wear, a new pair of hiking boots. At one time, he came to me and wanted my sales staff in Europe to help him get some literature across the borders of Europe marked as data sheets. I asked why he didn't just mail them and he told me that it was propaganda that was illegal to transport into western European nations. Needless to say, I wanted no part of that.

Rod and Steve shared the belief that salespeople were of little consequence in the scheme of business. In time, I did make a friend out of Rod, however. At one point, Apple had a problem with a semiconductor used to control the keyboard of the Apple II. It would fail in the field after a short period of time. Since it was a National Semiconductor product that I had been marketing before leaving, I knew exactly what the problem was, but he wasn't interested in hearing about it until it became a major problem in the field. One day he called me into a meeting with the National Semiconductor sales reps and said "Tell them what you told me about that component." I repeated that the parts needed some additional testing at temperature – called hot railing – to eliminate the failure mode of this component before shipping them to us. Once that testing was implemented, we had no further problems. From then on I gained newfound respect from Rod and we became friends.

Other early employees were Daniel Kottke, Bill Hernandez, and two kids still in high school, Chris Espinosa and Randy Wiggington, both software geniuses. Both too young to drive! Also, Sue Espinosa, Chris' mother, was an early employee. All are in the first ten employees as I recall.

The early manufacturing was done on the kitchen table of Hildi Licht so they did not have a manufacturing facility per se. The boards were hand stuffed with components and then flow soldered off-site to complete the process. The Bandley Drive facility, Apple' corporate headquarters in Cupertino, California was mainly testing, shipping, and administrative office space.

Since Apple was the first desktop computer to have color, our first computer monitor was a standard color television set. At that time, it was considered a gimmick by the mainframe and minicomputer companies and was given little consideration as a competitor. Today, no computer monitor is without color. This was just another first among many, many firsts for Apple innovations.

Explaining a new concept –
The Personal Computer

In the early stage of developing the personal computer market, Apple advertisements pushed the concept of "the computer for the rest of us," meaning the non-engineer consumers. One of our first selling documents was a brochure that described the basic elements of a computer. I wrote a brochure entitled, "A Consumers Guide to Personal Computers." It described the component parts as a central processor unit (CPU), information storage devices (memory), the data bus that connected the CPU to the memory, the input/output (I/O) bus that connected the CPU to the keyboard, and the display (TV screen) and/or a printer. It described what a personal computer could do and who would use it. Very basic information but needed for this new marketplace. This brochure became a major selling piece for those people new to the personal computer revolution that was just beginning.

Defining the Personal Computer concept

While giving seminars to prospective customers and dealers on the development of the Apple II and preaching the gospel of personal computers, I would give a brief history of the evolution of computers and would point out that the first personal computer was the ENIAC (Electronic Numerical Integrator and Calculator) electronic digital computer created in 1946. It was the first personal computer because there was only one person that knew how to run it. This computer consisted of 19,000 vacuum tubes and hundreds of thousands of electronic parts. The mean time to failure (MTBF) was calculated in hours, not even in days.

The next major step in computing was the mainframe computer. Its roots go back to before the turn of the twentieth century. An amalgam of companies was formed at the start of the twentieth century called Computing Tabulating Recording Corporation (CTR) and renamed International Business Machines (IBM) in 1924. This was the beginning of the mainframe computer era. It is told that Tom Watson proclaimed in the early days that there probably wasn't a need for more than ten computers in the world. These giant machines took up rooms that required air conditioning to cool the computers since they used so much power. Only a few engineers were trained to operate them, limiting the access to computing capability. An engineer/scientist would prepare their project on punched cards (Hollerith) or punched paper tape and submit them to a mainframe specialist that would input the data to the computer and return a printout of the results. This was a time consuming process.

Once the efficiency of computer computations was recognized, the demand for computing power rose exponentially in a short period of time. To give computer access to a larger number of engineers and businesses, computer terminals were connected to the mainframe via a data bus making the mainframe available to tens of people at a time.

In 1957, Ken Olson, an MIT graduate, and Harlan Anderson founded Digital Equipment Corporation in an old woolen mill in Massachusetts. He created a Mini Computer; smaller and more affordable than a mainframe, that could be accessed by hundreds of people. A minicomputer also required much less power since they used the new semiconductor technology being created at that time. Eventually, these machines became so popular that there were thousands of engineers and businesses that wanted access to a computer. This resulted in the development of networks of terminals, printers, and communication equipment that were connected together – via a data bus – for use throughout a company. This wide use of terminals created a new problem. If one of the terminals was shut off inadvertently, it closed down the whole bus system. This is where Dale Mrazek's Tri-State Logic invention previously mentioned came in to play. It was necessary to find a way to connect all of these terminals without conflicts occurring at the main computer.

By the 1970s thousands of engineers and scientists were hungry for greater access to a computer and a whole new era in computer technology erupted. Remember the axiom, *"necessity is the mother of invention?"* The outgrowth of that need was the creation of the Personal Computer industry. There were dozens of companies trying to fill this need. The most prominent in the mid 1970's were the PET Computer introduced by a calculator company called Commodore, the TRS-80 created by Radio Shack, and the Apple II Computer by Apple Computer, Inc. The Sol, the Osborne and a slew of other entrants followed these company computer offerings into this new market. As in all new industries, they were winnowed down to only a few.

The Apple Computer Coming Out Party

In June 1978, the annual computer conference for all computer and peripherals manufacturers was held in Anaheim, California. It was time for Apple to let the world know they existed. Apple signed up for booth space at the conference. We bought white sweaters and I had chenille Apple logos created in the six colors to put on the white sweater to identify the Apple representatives in the booth, and we were ready to make our move.

Personal computers were considered irrelevant in the eyes of the mainframe and minicomputer manufacturers that controlled the conference. They considered these computers with color TV displays mere toys. The convention management put us in the basement of the convention center. With low ceilings and noisy air conditioning equipment to contend with, we weren't in the best of places.

This was *not* what we wanted. We used the adage I coined at Fairchild Semiconductor, *"if you can't fix it, feature it."* We prepared some great flyers to hand out on the main floor and passed them out to anyone that would take one. By the second day, we had overwhelmed the information desk with requests for, "Where is the Apple booth?" and the convention management put up signs pointing to our space. We were a smash hit at that convention.

Beginning to Create a Sales Organization

This was where the fun began for me. There was no roadmap or history for reference to tell how to sell personal computers on a commercial basis. We had to define the mission and create the organization and sales channel that would be used to sell our products as we went along. We were charting new territory, which was an exciting challenge.

Our target customers in the beginning were largely engineers that wanted a computer on their desk, i.e., a *Personal Computer*.

Our first sales outlets were computer stores that were cropping up around the country. When we began looking for sales outlets in 1977, there were about twenty computer stores identified, most of which were called Byte Shops, and a franchise of electronic parts stores across the northern part of the U.S. called Team Electronics.

Let me digress for a moment. In 1976, the Byte Shop in Mountain View, California, placed an order for fifty Apple I computers with the two Steves. That was the beginning of Apple Computer, Inc.

To raise money to finance this *big* order for Apple I motherboards, Jobs sold his car and Woz sold his HP scientific calculator to buy the components for these boards. They would eventually build about fifty of these primitive systems, kind of a kit approach to building a computer.

The Apple II that succeeded this primitive machine was integrated into a case containing the keyboard, power supply, and memory along with card slots to accommodate the addition of specialized peripherals. Connecting a monitor to this case would provide a fully functional computer.

In addition to the Byte Shops there was also a department store in Toronto, Canada called Harts Department Store that had bought a quantity of Apple I boards. They were not terribly successful at selling this primitive form of a computer. This small group of computer enthusiasts was the basis for our initial computer store sales outlets.

When I approached them about carrying the new Apple II, I found resistance to the new machine since very few Apple I boards had sold through to end customers. In order to get the stores to stock the Apple II, we agreed to take back the Apple I on a one-for-one basis for each Apple II ordered. We got back several machines, some of them built into a brief case or into a box with the power supply and keyboard installed. We tossed them in the back room and eventually destroyed them.

In 2009, an Apple I sold on eBay for $16,000 and in 2010 one that came with a sales receipt signed by Steve Jobs sold for $213,000. In 2012, another one sold for $374,500 at a Sotheby auction. Another was reportedly sold in May 2013 in Germany by auction team Breker for $671,000. In 2014 Bonhams Auction House sold the latest Apple I for $905,000, a new record to date. Perhaps we were a little hasty in our destruction process.

Dealer training begins

In the late summer of 1977, Mike Markkula and I traveled to Minneapolis, Minnesota – the corporate headquarters of Team Electronics – to train about twenty of their most advanced dealers whose stores were situated across the northwestern U.S. Mike prepared a four-page brochure to introduce our product that stated, "Simplicity is the Ultimate Sophistication." On the front cover was a big picture of a Delicious apple (the 6 color apple logo had not yet been finished.) At the bottom it said Introducing Apple II – The Personal Computer. This brochure was our first piece of literature and today is a collector's item. I had twenty tee shirts printed with the words Apple II and a big Delicious apple in the center. This became the first of many many tee shirts created to announce a new product, application, or event at Apple Computer. So many in fact that a book by Gordon Thygeson, *Apple Tee Shirts*, was published on the history of each shirt.

Distributors and Dealers

As business increased, the next issue for a new company was the distribution of products around the world, and management of our accounts receivables. We also needed help in identifying and servicing the rapid growth of new computer dealers that were opening up across the U.S. and the world. We contracted with regional electronic distributors to help us identify and recommend dealers within their region for approval by Apple.

New dealers were required to meet the guidelines we defined to become an *Authorized Apple Dealer*. Further, the regional distributors helped us schedule our manufacturing line by ordering computers in relatively large volumes and reduced the number of companies that our credit department had to approve for credit and support. They also provided warehousing, local service centers, and distribution of our products in locations outside of California and reduced the shipping times for new orders. These multiple locations required a lot of travel for me since I was the only sales person for the first nine months of Apples existence. Branching out worldwide, we added a distributor in Japan and one in Europe. The European distributor – Eurapple – also created the interface for a European TV compatible version of the Apple II for sale in Europe.

As a new industry, it was important to maintain the quality of the dealer network as the sales channel grew. Sales techniques, service and support, and store presence in a city, were important to our image and each dealer had to meet certain standards to be authorized by Apple Computer. They signed a contract in which they agreed to abide by our guidelines for selling and servicing our products. There were no industry standards or guidelines to follow in managing this new sales outlet so it was made an annual contract. Each year the dealer agreements, if necessary, could be modified and each dealer was asked to requalify as an Authorized Dealer. If there were guidelines that needed to be updated or modified, they could be changed at this time. If the dealer was not living by these guidelines, they could be terminated without cause. We demanded a high quality of customer support, training, and repair from them in order to maintain a positive customer presence and an image of high quality equipment.

As the company grew over the next three years, the dealer channel grew from the twenty or so dealers initially, to over two thousand dealers in the U.S. alone by 1983. Sales became so brisk that we outstripped the ability of our distributors to service the dealer base effectively and it became necessary to take control of our sales effort directly in 1981.

With a lot of help from my first hire, Ron Rohner, Apple began building a sales team of manufacturers representatives – independent organizations that have a staff of people who are both competent technically and business savvy salespeople. We required Field Support Engineers be put on staff to help the customer configure his or her system to their needs. They were our independent sales team and were paid a commission on every sale they made. This kept our selling costs down since we paid for *sales* and not for employees. Apple constituted more than ninety percent of their sales so we had the complete attention of their representatives as well as their business. This was very lucrative for them and very cost effective for us. Our sales and distribution costs were less than ten percent in 1983.

Defining Sales Management

The next step was to create a field sales management team. Six area managers were hired over a short period of time. We had four U.S. area managers: East, South, Midwest, and West. In addition, we had a Far East manager and a Canadian manager. Europe was set up as an operations division with a full complement of management. This gave me an opportunity to bring in talent and expertise that I did not have. I looked for sales expertise in computer systems, computer products distribution, semiconductor sales, and international sales to help create a sales team that could provide expertise in all aspects of the selling process in this new consumer computer marketplace. There was no existing path to follow. We were blazing a new sales trail.

The first sales management meeting with the new area managers was held in Dallas, Texas, to introduce everyone and to put together a sales strategy. I told this new group that they had the opportunity to be part of a very exciting new business. It would be the experience of a lifetime and we had to move fast. To make my point, I wore a pair of cowboy boots and put my feet on the table and told them that I would be out there kicking ass and taking names if they weren't giving 110 percent. If they found that it was too hard or they didn't like it, find another job so I didn't have to fire them.

They all bought in to the program and understood the message. Before long, I started receiving all forms of cowboy boots: brass boots, pictures of boots, wooden boot art, etc., as souvenirs from these managers. The one I cherish the most is a brass etching of a boot inscribed, "You made it happen," with the signature of each area manager. They bought me a pair of alligator boots for my birthday that was celebrated during a sales meeting in San Diego. The word got back to the human resources manager and I was visited by her telling me that such talk was inappropriate in a business. It was effective and everyone knew how I stood. The IBM sales manager I hired to run the Dallas office was generally at odds with our selling process in the beginning because it didn't follow the mainframe concept. Years later, he paid me a compliment by telling me how much he enjoyed his relationship with Apple. Thirty plus years later, in 2011, one of the original members of the management team emailed me thanks for giving him the chance of a lifetime by being a part of the Apple adventure. I think they enjoyed the journey.

These managers hired and managed the manufacturers representatives that sold our products in their region. Our field sales organization grew to over a thousand members who managed the computer dealers around the world by 1983.

Challenges of managing a fast growing business

This fast growth along with the dealer stores of the time created another problem/opportunity. That was credit worthiness of these dealers. Many of them had an individual net worth of less than $50,000. These same people were buying Apple IIs four or eight at a time with little or no credit record. The credit department often blocked a shipment of systems to a dealer because of their credit worthiness. After much gnashing of teeth by the sales team, I made a deal with our CFO. Every finance department has a bad debt allowance built into their plan. Our CFO, Ken Zerbe, agreed to give the sales department a bad debt allowance and as long as the bad debt stayed below a predefined figure cumulatively, I had the power to approve shipments to dealers with questionable credit history. We did that by giving seven-day, fourteen-day, or thirty-day terms depending on credit history and their conformance to the credit terms at each level of purchases. A dealer could earn longer terms by paying on time. We never overextended our credit limit and the arrangement allowed Apple to grow a dealer channel of small business entrepreneurs while expanding sales that grew by double and triple digit percentages in the next seven years.

In another innovation, Ron Rohner set up a financing plan for the dealers created around the auto dealers' financing plan called "flooring". The dealer would buy the machines funded by General Electric Credit Corporation (GECC) and then would pay a finance charge each month that their stock was unsold after purchase. This was another way for the larger dealers to keep supplies of machines in their stores.

Inside Sales

During this growing time, we needed product literature, dealer advertising and customer support training on the products from product marketing. It didn't happen. The Apple II marketing manager was recruited from Intel. Intel marketing people were product *managers* and not product *marketers*. He had no experience in developing product marketing materials. At Intel, these product managers were technically competent and did sales support from the factory. They were not schooled in the development of collateral marketing and sales support material.

I lobbied Mike Markkula to recruit Phil Roybal from National Semiconductor to do the product marketing of our products. I prevailed and Phil joined Apple in January 1978. While he reported to the marketing department, he worked with me to create dealer and customer marketing support and technical material. He was an incredible addition to our support staff. I will add more on Phil later.

After an extended period of time begging for product marketing support materials, I said we would create our own product literature, advertising promotions, and training support materials. Steve Jobs protested saying that sales people were not competent to be marketing people. (Recall that he told me that the only people that go into sales are those that are too dumb to do anything else.) So, I created a department within the sales department for sales support and we called it *Inside Sales*. The inside sales department grew to about 120 people strong and specialized in sales support, industry centric support materials, dealer advertising materials, and training materials for all of these various sales groups that included education, industrial, corporate, and dealer support.

The sales department played off the corporate advertising campaign that was developed by the advertising manager, Fred Hoar. When asked how to spell his name, being a glib man with a sense of humor he would say F-R-E-D. It was important that we know what ads they were preparing so we could take advantage of the message when it was announced in the press. I asked to be involved in the design and concept of the ads being created. Since that had been my responsibility at National Semiconductor, I wanted an input into their creation. In keeping with the Steve Jobs feeling about sales people, Fred stonewalled me until one day he agreed to let me see an ad for the Apple /// – "but you can't change anything in the content." When I got through reading the ad, I said it was pretty good but it had a misspelled word in it. The word was "hierarchical" and not hierarchal. From then on I got to see the ads before they went out and was allowed to comment on their content. We sales people have to prove ourselves every step of the way.

Major Events of Early Apple

Most of these events are available on the Internet but in a variety of web locations. These stories are the *behind the scenes* escapades that drove the major announcements of our company.

Apple Core

Since, the only application we had at the beginning was a BASIC programming language and the Checkbook application that Mike Markkula had written, we needed application programs to display the capabilities of the machines. Sales started a newsletter called the *Apple Core* that was sent out each month to the dealers. We included updates on what was going on at Apple and tech notes. We also paid a $25 honorarium for any program developed by new Apple users that were sent in to us for distribution. We received a lot of small programs that were useful to our new customers and dealers. My son was fifteen and worked the summer debugging these programs so we could distribute them.

Establishing the new fiscal year

Apple started shipping product in August 1977 and sold about $70,000 worth of products in the first two months. A new company is allowed to change their fiscal year once and it was decided that our fiscal year should end September 30. Our first full year of sales was about $700,000. The next was about $7,000,000 and we grew quickly from there to achieve sales of $984 million in fiscal 1983.

The first Apple Christmas party

By the end of 1977, there were approximately thirty-five employees. We decided to have a Christmas party at the Blue Pheasant restaurant in Cupertino, California. It was to be a semi-formal event in keeping with a growing business. Steve Jobs was informed that Levis and sandals were not appropriate evening wear to which he violently disagreed. He came to the Christmas party in tuxedo tails, a red bowtie over a white tee shirt, and red tennis shoes.

The first company picnic

The first company picnic was held in our back yard in July 1978. I remember that the engineers just kind of sat around and watched while the marketing folks partied. A good time was had by all.

Programming and data management

Prior to the advent of disk drives, an audio cassette player was utilized for loading the operating system software and the few application programs that were available. This was a tedious and time-consuming job. There was no way to save data from the computer so it had to be loaded on to the machine each time you powered up. It took several minutes to load and was *not* a selling feature of the machine. We needed a fix for this effort.

Recall that Phil Roybal joined Apple from National Semiconductor in January of 1978. He had a degree in Computer Science and an oratorical gift. One of his first projects was to create a sales tool to be used in demonstrating the features of the Apple II utilizing this cassette player. Phil developed a taped presentation and a running dialog to be used by the store personnel to keep the customer occupied during the three or four minute loading process. We also needed a means to save the computational results developed on the computer.

The Floppy Disk Drive

In late 1977, Shugart Associates showed us a new storage device they had developed called the floppy disk drive. It was a disk drive that accepted a 5¼" flexible diskette that could read and write 144,000 bytes of data from, or on to, the disk. This is a drop in the bucket by today's standards but a major breakthrough in technology in 1977. You may recall that I said I had been privileged to be associated with two of the most talented engineers of our time. Steve Wosniak was one of them. Woz got a sample drive from Shugart on Thanksgiving weekend, 1977. In the course of the next six weeks, he designed the hardware interface for the Apple II as well as the software to control the disk (called the disk operating system (DOS). This is an incredible feat of engineering for one man to undertake. It was estimated to be a four to six man-year job in a normal design cycle. We were able to demonstrate the disk drive operating at the Consumer Electronics Show (CES) in Las Vegas on January 6, 1978, less than two months after he started the design. Apple Computer was the hit of the show.

The Consumer Electronic Show; January 1978

The Consumer Electronics Show is the major consumer product selling venue held each year in Las Vegas, Nevada, in early January. Thousands of dealers and buyers attend this show and it was the first major event for Apple. We rented the only floor space available in the convention center. It was among the watch manufacturers. Since there was no computer industry at this time, we took space wherever there was room for us. I bought a bookcase from a Swedish furniture store that came knocked down and that became our backdrop for the booth. Sue Cabaniss, our purchasing manager, pulled a U-Haul trailer full of our equipment to Las Vegas. Steve Jobs and I flew in later to set up the booth. Steve, Mike Markkula and I stood booth duty from nine to six, answering thousands of questions from curious attendees while our wives passed out literature to passersby. Mike had written a program to use the computer as a checkbook ledger for keeping track of your household budget. That was about the extent of the software, other than a BASIC programming language that engineers could use to write their own programs. These were exhausting days, but it was so thrilling to be part of a new industry that no one complained.

An anecdote: Steve Jobs and I were the two that set up our booth on the exhibition floor at the CES show. Steve irritated the union people by doing some of the work they should have done because we couldn't get them to bring our equipment to the floor. To get even, they brought our equipment from the loading dock last to punish us for doing *their* job. It was 2 A.M. when Steve and I got back to our motel. There was Woz, in my room working feverishly on the DOS software for the disk drive. He said his wife was sleeping in his room and she wanted it quiet. I told him, rather indelicately, to get out of my room because I had to stand booth duty at 9 A.M. and needed some sleep.

The Apple II disk drive introduction

The disk drive was a major breakthrough for personal computers to have built-in storage ability. We had promised to deliver first products to the dealers by June 30 for July introduction. The last days were "panicsville" but we were committed to making our date. The night of June 30 every employee, wife of employee, son and daughter, and the warehouse staff formed a production line to pack the devices for shipment to meet our promised deadline. At about 1 A.M. "June 31," we completed our task and were ready for the delivery service to pick them up first thing in the morning. MISSION ACCOMPLISHED! This is the fun of being part of a start-up company. Everyone and anyone got involved when necessary.

Apple introduced the Disc II with a promotional price of $495 because we didn't know how many we would sell. We way under forecasted the demand and were overbooked within a few weeks of introduction.

When our purchasing agent went to Shugart and told them we needed four thousand drives a month they said *no way*! They couldn't build that many and we couldn't possibly sell that many. But we did. It wasn't long before Alps, a Japanese company, became a vendor of the drive for us.

The Apple Road Show

In April and May of 1981 Bob Rogers, Ron Rohner, Don Williams, and Phil Roybal devised the Apple Road Show to blitz the personal computer industry. We set a tour of four cities: Dallas, Chicago, New York and Los Angeles, in five weeks to promote, train, and educate our dealers, sales people, and customers on all that was Apple. Two semitrailer trucks transported the equipment between locations. They were painted with big Apple logos proclaiming "Apple Expo" on the side and would come into the city like the Barnum and Bailey Circus with great fanfare. We would travel on Sunday and set up on Monday. There were 26 seminars and a trade show in each city. The dealer days brought dealers up-to-date on new products through six concurrent "how-to" seminars in an Apple Pie setting in the round. The training consisted of sales, repair, accounting, product presentation, etc. in each "slice" of the pie every thirty minutes. Another day was for a public trade show exhibition. Apple field sales representatives and manufacturers representatives were trained on the computer and applications software on another day. Friday was open to consumers and prospective new dealers to visit the displays. We had long lines of people queuing up early to get into these events in each city. The press would be briefed and we would tear down on Friday afternoon, traveling home Friday night. It was a huge promotional success but pretty hard on the sales team.

Developing a Department and Corporate Philosophy

Early in the Apple Computer culture, each department was asked to create a philosophy doctrine for their department. It was a good way to foster a corporate wide mentality for how the company should conduct business and how departments were expected to interact. It was also an excellent way to communicate to all field sales personnel how we expected our customers to be treated. The following was the sales philosophy contribution.

The Apple Sales Philosophy

Dale Carnegie once remarked that money buys but enthusiasm sells. Our strongest asset is the enthusiasm that surrounds the Apple Selling Process. Maintaining that enthusiasm from the personnel who design and manufacture the product, to the customer who buys it, is what has made us a success. The sales division is dedicated to providing a creative environment that will keep the selling process fun. Keeping it fun must be maintained at almost any cost if we are to preserve our competitive edge with the dealer base and the customer.

There are three elements in the selling process: a need, a solution, and a means of combining the two. In order to assist someone it is necessary to know their need or problem, have the right solution for the problem, and be able to communicate the solution at the customers' level of comprehension. The customer must feel the solution provided is of equal value to the fee paid.

The selling process begins with communications. The company provides solutions to problems with the products they manufacture. Visualize the sales division as a conduit of information. They must listen to the customers needs and recommend a solution (product) to fill that need. The quality of the communication is dependent upon the training and product knowledge given to the salesperson.

The selling process is a team effort with participation by everyone in the company. Technical leadership, quality of merchandise, availability of product, and training of the salespeople are important in closing the sale.

13

Going Public: December 12, 1980

Apple Computer sales had gone very well and the company was in need of cash. Rather than take additional venture capital, which would dilute our share of the company, it was decided to go public. The major investment banker was Morgan Stanley. The initial public offering (IPO), initially scheduled for $14 to $17, was established at introduction to be $22.00. The stock closed the trading day at $28.50. The place was delirious on that day.

There was a celebration dinner for the Apple executive staff and the investment-banking firm. At this dinner, the Morgan Stanley staff challenged us to a foot race, probably after too much wine. We accepted the challenge. This was not *just* a foot race, it was the annual Bay to Breakers Race, 7.62 miles from San Francisco Bay to the Pacific Ocean! It is an annual San Francisco event that occurs in May. We had about five months to prepare. None of us had run more than a mile as part of our exercise regimen so it was a challenge we shouldn't have undertaken. About ten or fifteen of us took on the challenge. I was doing fine until we got to the Hays Street hill, about halfway through the course. The

Hays Street hill did me in. As I walked instead of ran up the hill, my leg muscles knotted up and cramped. I didn't think I could make it to the end and decided to take a cab to the finish line. *Big* problem. I was wearing a tee shirt, shorts and running shoes! I had no money or identification. Consequently I had to finish the race. It was about three days before I could get out of a chair without help! I still have the tee shirt we were given for the accomplishment as a symbol of my effort.

Personal Computer applications software development.

The event that really put the personal computer on the map was the development of the first spreadsheet application. Dan Bricklin and Bob Frankston formed Software Arts and wrote the VISICALC spreadsheet for personal computers. It was first announced on the Apple II in 1979, and later on other machines. This opened up a whole new market for the personal computer. Sales and marketing could create business plans, design engineers could do math intensive design analyses, and management could run financial analyses of their business. It was a game changer in our industry.

Initial word processing was available in the form of a text editor. The first word processing was done on a monitor with only forty characters/line. That is a half page width display. Eventually, we added an eighty-column card, for full-page display capability to the computer and a monitor that could display it. Then you could see what a printed page was going to look like. This word processing capability was instrumental in replacing the typewriter with a personal computer. That moved us another step forward in the personal computer development. The industry now had a display with *What You See Is What You Get* or WYSIWYG capability. The page layout on the computer screen is what will be printed.

But it was the spreadsheet that opened up the plethora of new ideas and concepts. Recall my hand written spreadsheets for the National Semiconductor business plan 1974. I immediately realized what a godsend this applications would have been in that application.

The Apple ///

VISICALC single handedly jump-started the use of the Apple II as a personal computer. It also made us realize the shortcomings of the Apple II in a business environment. The development of the Apple /// was started to address the business market. It was obvious that a floppy disk drive that could only store 144 kilobytes of data was insufficient for a business application. About the same time, Seagate developed a 5¼-inch hard disk drive that could store five megabytes of information. This was sufficient for use in a business application and the Apple /// was introduced in May 1980.

Apple Means Business

In the mid 1970s, National Semiconductor created a marketing and advertising program called "The System Sell." Instead of selling individual components, National began selling a design concept declaring they had the components for every design need. The ad listed all of the components available on one page by function. This was a very powerful promotional method because it helped the engineer find most of their component parts from one vendor.

Small businesses became interested in personal computers as a cost effective way of managing their business. Peripherals were becoming available and accounting software packages were developed for the Apple ///. Now we could sell a complete system.

In the early 1980s, Apple used this system sell concept to develop a similar plan for the small business market. The promotional material proclaimed *Apple Means Business*. We put together a complete bundled package – computer, peripherals, modem, printer, and accounting software – to support this advertising program.

Apple put on seminars all over the country demonstrating how an Apple /// business system works. They could run their entire business using the modem to interconnect the company's computers for communication (this was pre- Internet), high-speed business printer, a hard drive for applications software and data storage, and Great Plains Accounting Software. It was only moderately successful but it did introduce a wake up call to IBM and other large computer companies.

The Apple /// was rushed to completion for Apple's trip to the National Computer Conference at Anaheim, California in May 1980. The operating system wasn't ready, the hardware wasn't ready, but it was released prematurely. Most of the machines were recalled and it was a marketing disaster. It was reintroduced in the fall as the Apple ///+. In 1981, IBM introduced their line of personal computers labeled the "PC" because Apple had trademarked the phrase "Personal Computer". It did, however, validate the use of personal computers in industry. Apple produced an ad simply saying "WELCOME IBM" seriously! Hardware glitches eventually caused the demise of the machine and a temporary blemish on the quality of Apple products.

Meanwhile, the Apple II division continued to develop new products: the Apple II+, the Apple IIe, and in 1983, a quasi-portable Apple IIc which had a semi-round shape. It became known as the toilet seat computer. It was important that Apple continue to create new Apple II models because these products were paying the bills for the development of the next generation of computers – the Lisa and Macintosh.

Betting the Company: The development of the Lisa Computer; a giant step in the development of the modern Personal Computer

Steve Jobs heard about a computer development at the Xerox Research Center in Palo Alto (called PARC), a research and development lab for Xerox Corporation that seldom commercialized their concepts. They had designed a computer they called the ALTO computer that used a bit-mapped display that led to the development of a plethora of character fonts: graphical user interface (GUI), an object oriented programming language called Small Talk – that simplified software development – and a mouse as a pointing device. Steve got very excited about this concept and asked if Apple could license the technology. Xerox agreed, if we would accept their retail outlet printer stores as Apple Computer dealers. He agreed immediately and came back and informed me that I was to include the Xerox stores as part of our dealer channel. The development of the Lisa computer began.

This was a bet-the-company type of decision in that Lisa strayed from the concept of the Apple II and the Apple ///. It was also going to be a very expensive development for a young company to fund. It was to be a new business system concept for personal computers using Lisa as a *mainframe* with satellite intelligent terminals. An office could be managed with a Lisa and several intelligent remotes in a network; the Macintosh was a prototype of this concept and was in the design phase in a different division.

Lisa required some advanced development techniques to make it a viable office computer. The existing 140-kilobyte storage floppy disk was not sufficient storage for an office system so an engineering project began the development of a 640-kilobyte floppy disk drive under John Vennard. This increase in density challenged the read/write head technology and the speed that the disk had to spin. The higher speed proved to create a problem resulting from the heat generated by the drive. The extra speed required a different disk lubricant. The difficulties with the development subsequently resulted in a lawsuit that found Mike Markkula and John Vennard personally liable for its failure. Fortunately, the courts later set this ruling aside. It was these kinds of innovative advanced developments that moved technology forward. Unfortunately, some did not achieve their desired results.

It was about this time, 1982-83 that hard disk drives were becoming of physical and memory density size to make them compatible with desktop computers. Early hard drives were the size of a desk. Again, *necessity is the mother of invention,* and the new computer concepts were bringing the size down to meet the needs of the personal computer. The Lisa was first sold with a five-megabyte hard drive that had been developed for the Apple /// business system. Today a normal hard drive is two terabytes or more requiring only a small portion of the physical space of that first drive.

The software was also a new innovation. The Lisa operating system provided multitasking capability; it could do multiple functions simultaneously. The application software was an early example of the Microsoft Office Suite that later became the industry standard for personal computer applications software.

The Lisa Sales Challenge

This project was a very secret development and required a different sales organization from that of the Apple II and Apple ///. It was to a different customer and at a much higher price point. The Apple II was about $1200 and the Lisa was $10,000. This is comparable to asking a Honda salesman to sell a Mercedes Benz automobile! Being highly secret, the field staff was given about six weeks to identify, select, and train a group of Apple dealers on how to sell this product.

The sales personnel mounted a valiant attempt and many companies embraced the concept but Apple was not successful in making a market for this machine.

There was a lot of discussion around the industry that Apple had failed in this project. I saw it in a different light. The Alto sold for about $50,000. Lisa sold for $10,000 and its successor; the Macintosh sold for $2,500. In any new market, the first evolution always costs more to design and build. Without the interim development of the Lisa technology, the next evolution of this concept in desktop computing might never have seen the light of day – the Macintosh. The success of the Macintosh certainly validated the effort that was put into this new concept in personal computing.

The Macintosh Computer – the machine for the rest of us

The Macintosh Development

Steve Jobs was devastated when he wasn't chosen to manage the Lisa project. He felt that it was his project – perhaps rightly so – and that he should be the general manager of the division. As I said, this was a *bet-the-company* decision to embark on the project. Steve was in his early 20's with no management experience or people skills and was deemed not ready to lead by the executive staff of the company.

During this time, we had a skunkworks project going on in an off-site facility chartered with designing and building what was called a computer appliance – a machine that would do all things for all people using the Graphical User Interface (GUI), a mouse pointing device, multitasking operating system, and the newly created hierarchical file system of Lisa but on a much smaller and less costly scale. This project was under the direction of Jeff Raskin. Jeff had a Ph.D. in Engineering and had been hired to write the manuals for the Apple II and Apple *///*. He devised the concept of a small computer that would be designed off the Lisa design but at one-fourth the price. He envisioned an *appliance* for the home like a toaster or a blender or other household items.

Steve decided that if he couldn't run the Lisa project, he would take over the Macintosh project and pushed Jeff out. This became the skunkworks that operated on the fringes of Apple like pirates at sea. Matter of fact, they flew a skull and crossbones flag above their engineering building that was situated behind a Texaco gas station that became known as the Texaco Towers. Jeff would later write a book scornfully parroting the press that called Steve a visionary. Jeff said yes, he was a visionary who was "dragged kicking and screaming towards a new idea that he would eventually call his own."

This team of engineers was a team of young men and women with a shared vision who would create the Macintosh computer as it exists today, over 30 years later. The "Mac" set the standard for all future personal computers. This team of people were driven and worked long hours in the process of perfecting the concept they envisioned.

As the machine progressed in development, the Apple management staff eventually got their first look at it. This was to be the business machine market that Lisa had not penetrated. The price varied as new features came along. The first keyboard came without a ten key numeric pad and Steve would not budge saying it was not needed and would cost extra money. I jokingly said that I would start a business to build ten key numeric pad because a business office could not operate without a ten key pad. Another revelation that prompted my next *business opportunity* was that there was no accommodation for a hard drive. Steve said it was not necessary as long as we had a floppy disk drive built in.

A new floppy drive concept

The drive, a 5-1/4 inch floppy disk drive, was taking up too much room in the Macintosh case and the design team was trying to decide what to do about that issue. During the Consumer Electronic Show in Las Vegas in 1983, Sony introduced a new floppy disk that used a totally enclosed, 3½-inch diskette with 400 kilobytes of memory storage. I picked up a sample of the new technology to bring home to Steve and he scoffed at it. A few months later, he had an epiphany; he found this Sony disk drive that would be perfect for the Mac. You may recall that Jeff Raskin said Steve had to be dragged kicking and screaming to a new idea only to call it his own. That was the Steve Jobs way.

As the development progressed there was a push to announce the machine as soon as possible. After the premature announcement of the Apple ///, I was very concerned about rushing this machine to the market and brought it up at every staff meeting. Steve got a little upset with me and had a painting done by the advertising agency that played off a wine commercial of the time done by Orson Welles. He said in the commercial, "We will release no wine before its time." The Apple version of this painting says, "We will announce no Apple before its time." I cherished that painting because, after the Apple /// debacle, it was a constant reminder to everyone of the importance of being ready for a product introduction. It goes without saying that I also cherish it because it came from Steve Jobs.

The 1984 Macintosh Super Bowl Ad

Apple Computer had one of the premiere advertising agencies of the time, Chiatt/Day. This agency was incredibly creative. I had the privilege of working with them at National Semiconductor when I was the director of marketing. I made quarterly visits to their offices in Los Angeles to brainstorm new product ads with them. When we were preparing to introduce the Macintosh, they came up with a TV commercial to be viewed during the halftime of the Super Bowl. This commercial was a takeoff on the George Orwell book *1984* which described people as robots of the ruling junta. This was synonymous with how a major computer company controlled the thinking of most large corporations when it came to buying computers. The executive staff just about had heart failure when they first viewed the commercial. This was kind of like waving a red flag in front of a bull! We agreed that this was a big mistake and that the commercial should be cancelled. They had bought a sixty-second and a thirty-second spot during the Super Bowl that cost about $750,000. We told them to sell the spots. They supposedly tried but couldn't find any buyers at that late date so the ads went on. Long story short, the commercial was so successful that in 2011, twenty-seven years later, it was still voted the most famous commercial to ever show during a Super Bowl! Fortunately, the executive staff got outvoted and it ran.

Since the inception of the personal computer in the late 1970s, many different computer companies have competed for prominence in the marketplace. Apple Computer started the movement to desktop computers and copyrighted the phrase "personal computer" in 1977 with the introduction of the Apple II. In 1981, IBM claimed the invention of the personal computer and named it the PC because Apple had the rights to the name Personal Computer. Since then, many different companies have announced different versions using a Microsoft based operating system. Since the introduction of the Macintosh Computer incorporating a Graphical User Interface (GUI), mouse pointing device, and integrated software applications, it has been recognized as the leader in computer systems user interface. This GUI system was later adopted by Microsoft and has been the standard for all applications on both Apple and Microsoft compatible personal computers.

Selling to the Industry Market Segments

As the product lines expanded and with the proliferation of personal computers, additional sales functions had to be added to take advantage of this in the multiple market complex that was expanding beyond dealer sales. The synergism between dealer sales and industry sales was a challenge that had to be addressed carefully. Some enterprising dealers had formed outside sales teams to increase their sales reach. When Apple started direct sales, it was necessary to keep everyone happy with the new process. Each segment provided a new challenge.

The dealer channel

For the first three years of Apple's existence, the dealers were our strategic partners and primary sales outlets. They were our primary concern for training and support. Twice a year a conference was convened that brought invited dealers to Cupertino to discuss issues and strategies that affected our selling process and their businesses. Many of the dealers were experienced business people and we gained as much from them as they did from us in these weeklong conferences.

With the introduction of the IBM PC in 1981 and their validation of the industry, everything began to change. Personal computing was still our major emphasis but the marketplace was changing by the day. New software applications for a personal computer were being devised in every business environment.

Apple Computers in the school

First let me add a little history on the Apple involvement in computers in schools. It had always been our intent to introduce personal computers into the school system. In the late 1970s, there were about 103,000 public schools that we could identify in the U.S. In the early days, 1977-78, when we were still a private company and struggling to increase sales of the Apple II, Steve Jobs conceived the idea to get an Apple II Computer placed in every school in the country. He wanted to donate a computer to every school: public and private, grade and high schools, and universities. He took this proposal to Washington and presented it to the Congressional leaders. He asked for a tax break for the cost of the parts for every machine we would donate. He was rebuffed saying that it was a gimmick to get our taxes down and said that every other company would want the same deal. One Congressman asked him "What's your game kid?" Educational sales were always a major part of the Apple sales objective, then and now.

Despite being rebuffed by the government, we did however begin working with schools. Bell and Howell was a company that sold movie projectors, slide projectors and other audio/visual equipment to all levels of schools. We developed a distribution arrangement with them to sell the Apple II into these educational institutions, using their established sales organization. Their equipment was all black so we developed a line of "black Apples" for their sales channel. They were instrumental in getting our products introduced to a large school audience. In time, it became evident that their sales people were primarily order takers. By that I mean that they didn't sell the machines, they took orders for them if asked. They didn't have the technical skillset to present the capabilities of the machine. Their sales organization began selling outside their designated channel, which was in conflict with our other businesses as well as our business agreement. We decided it was time to create our own educational sales team.

There were school districts like Cupertino, California, Dallas, Texas, and a Minnesota Consortium of schools that were progressive in establishing computers in the classroom. In the first endeavor into schools, we learned from helping the nearby Cupertino School District set up computer labs in some of their schools.. Later, a school district in Dallas, Texas, also progressive in establishing computers in the classroom, became the next big customer followed by the Minneapolis Educational Computer Consortium (MECC). The trend for computers in the school continues to grow in size thirty years later. Now it is the iPads and other tablets that are gaining popularity today.

By 1982 we began building a direct sales team that called on the school districts of major cities. With four sales representatives, we set a goal of five million dollars in sales for the first year. This was a modest goal, but starting from scratch we had no idea how large this market could become. We achieved that goal in the first year and doubled the goal for the next year and achieved that goal as well. Small numbers compared to todays sales but nonetheless significant at the time. It was the basis for what is today a very large market for Apple Computer.

Establishing National Accounts Sales

With the advent of the Lisa computer, we started hiring sales representatives in 1981 to call on Fortune 500 companies. This was mildly successful but we were again battling the mainframe vendors. With a small sales team selling to schools and another to Fortune 500 companies, we continued to expand with the majority of our sales coming from our dealer base. It created a conflict between direct sales and dealer directed sales that caused some issues that had to be ironed out. With about 2500 authorized dealers from the 20+ we started with four years earlier, we were challenged to be sure that the customer was supported properly. It was, however, necessary for us to make contact with large corporate customers to determine their needs in anticipation of the new concept in personal computing that the Lisa computer presented. With the first ever integrated software capability, hard disk drive storage and enhanced computing power, this machine was a new challenge that the sales team was not prepared to deal with. It was a different design concept than the Apple II and Apple /// and it was much more expensive and a more powerful machine. It was not Apple's most successful product but it did move the evolving personal computer industry forward to the concept of GUI interface, integrated applications, and operating system software that would be introduced on the less expensive Macintosh a couple of years later.

Supporting the Industrial Customer

By 1981, the personal computer had become ubiquitous. There were opportunities for small applications in a plethora of industrial applications and it was our responsibility to find solutions, either through software or hardware, before we could take our place in that market. Previously application-specific computers were being designed for each application. Now standard computers using software/hardware interfaces could do a job more economically and complete the design phase quicker. The Apple II had eight card slots on an S-100 bus to accommodate custom designed interface solutions, and specialized computers were no longer required. This was another industry specific sales opportunity to be addressed.

With this new concept in computer usage, Apple began hiring field systems engineers to work with the customer base in the design of their projects to augment those on the manufacturers representatives' staff. This was the next generation of field applications engineers that were introduced by National Semiconductor and Intel Corporation in the developing integrated circuit designs of the 1970s.

Corporate sales, education sales, industrial sales, and dealer sales all required a different level of expertise or a different approach in the selling process. This was the challenge and the exciting part of the personal computer business. In deference to Steve Jobs, sales organizations are an integral part of any corporate team selling new ideas to industry.

The Changing of the Guard
and Corporate Vision

John Sculley joins Apple Computer

After the departure of Mike Scott in 1981, Apple began a search for a new CEO. The search identified John Sculley, president of Pepsi Cola in early 1983. He had marketing skills in consumer products and an interest in electronics. Steve Jobs was sent to New York for several weekends to brief him on Apple and for the two to get to know each other.

In April 1983 John Sculley was appointed CEO of Apple Computer. The press proclaimed, or someone told the press, that he was brought in to bring "adult supervision" to Apple. I guess that is what you call corporate bureaucracy and office politics. There was more than enough competency in the management team that "adult supervision" was not necessary. It soon became obvious that his vision and my vision for Apple did not coincide. We had some philosophical difference confrontations that made me realize that if the vice president of sales had conflicts with the CEO, the only loser would be the VP of Sales. For example, our cost of sales, including the distribution of product, was about seven percent of sales during my tenure. John Sculley was determined that Apple should have its own direct sales organization. I felt we had the best organization at the lowest costs of sales and defended that position vigorously. I fought that battle until I resigned in 1984. Three months after I resigned from Apple, the manufacturers representative sales team was disbanded by John Sculley and replaced by an Apple direct sales organization. The sales costs more than doubled in short order.

By early 1984 it was time to leave. I resigned my position as Sales VP in March and remained on in a nonoperational role for the next three months. I had seen the company grow from $0 to $984 million in just seven years. This was an accomplishment in anyone's world.

An Apple Computer Store Concept

One of the challenges for Apple was competing with IBM for sales time in the computer dealers' stores. We needed better representation in the stores for our share of personal computer sales. We also needed to train customers on how to use an Apple Computer since personal computers were new to the industry.

Bob Rogers, Ron Rohner and I had a vision of an Apple company store in our mind. Bob was a cofounder of Compushop, an early computer store in Dallas, Texas. Ron Rohner had previous experience in the consumer advertising and promotion business before joining Apple Computer. Competition for sales at the independent dealer level was not under our control and we were losing the "David vs. Goliath" battle with IBM. Funny how IBM is out of the personal computer business and Apple is in the personal electronics business today.

During that three month period after leaving the vice president of sales position, we, along with Jeff Barco and Linda Paulson, presented an Apple store concept to the Apple executive staff and were given the go-ahead to develop a business plan and build a prototype store. The concept was for a chain of stores supported by regional super stores that called for a main store "hub" in major population areas and satellite stores in cities in the surrounding area. This store concept could sell, train, repair and warehouse our products closer to the customer. For the next three months, we built a 3000 square foot prototype store. It would not have served us well for our existing dealers to know that we were planning on competing with them for sales so it was another skunkworks project built inside a warehouse in San Jose, California. The prototype was a complete store with display areas, training area, service area, and a point-of-sale system. On May 11, 1984, we presented our concept to the executive staff and after a short consideration, John Sculley decided that he didn't have time to worry about a new sales channel and the store concept was dropped. Today, we know that it was an idea that came before its time. Today the Apple Stores are the most successful sales outlets in the world comprising a major portion of their annual sales and selling more dollars of merchandise per square foot than any other business in the world.

With the conclusion of that project, I was no longer an Apple employee. This was a little jolting in that I had been going one hundred miles an hour for seven years and then abruptly stopped. Then fate stepped in and gave me other opportunities. Or was it being in the right place at the right time?

Vision and its effect on new ideas

Perhaps this is a time to talk about vision. It is interesting to note that so many old-line companies have missed the development of new technologies and new innovations. Doing what they do seems to blind them to a vision of a new industry or concept. Many of these new concepts could have been Fairchild Semiconductor or National Semiconductor or IBM or HP innovations but management didn't see it. New markets and design concepts are created by people with a vision of the future and willing to gamble on its success. The spin-offs from Fairchild were good examples. I was unsuccessful in getting National Semiconductor to build small computers. The two Steves tried to get a venture capitalist to fund Apple Computer and it was Mike Markkula who saw the vision of the personal computer and invested his time and money in that vision. Thankfully I was directed to Apple instead of the small computer I was trying to fund. Would we have been successful? Who knows?

Microsoft would probably not exist if IBM had had a vision for the importance of the operating system and had bought – instead of licensing – MS-DOS. With better vision, they may still be in the PC business.

HP had the vision for scientific calculators but didn't have a vision for small computers and is still trying to rebuild their brand.

Start-ups like Facebook, Instagram, Google, eBay, GoPro, Splunk, Yahoo, Tesla, Netflix and so many others were started by a person or group of people with a common vision of a new idea and were willing to gamble on its success. These innovations may never have been created if it was left up to the established, old-line companies to create these new enterprises, the basis for the electronic revolution we are experiencing.

Life Beyond Apple Computer

Generating an income stream

During the early eighties most of the early employees realized that our total net worth was tied up in Apple stock. This was a time when your financial rewards were in stock options and not in big salaries. Relying on selling stock for income could potentially be a problem. Short term, there were tax implications. Long term, you were selling off your stock investments that should/would create greater potential for financial gain. We began looking for some kind of investment that would generate cash flow from an investment that we could live on in the event we were not working.

In a conversation with one of my associates, John Couch, we talked about this situation. Again, either fate stepped in or it qualifies as good planning! John said he had been talking with a partnership group interested in finding investors to buy a landfill on the San Francisco Bay in San Jose.

The disposal of trash, garbage and building materials in metropolitan areas had become a major concern in a lot of cities around the country. Cities like San Francisco, California and New York, New York had to barge their waste materials away from the city. San Jose foresaw this becoming a problem for the south end of San Francisco Bay and began looking for alternatives.

The general partners were looking for investors to help them purchase an old landfill – a seventy-acre parcel on the south bay – that had been closed for several years. Their plan was to convert this property into a transfer station for sorting and processing building demolition debris and recyclable materials. The general partners, Rich Cristina and Murray Hall saw an opportunity to make a business of recycling building materials while reducing the amount of refuse that was buried in landfills. A group of Apple executives met with them, and in 1985, ten investors participated in the purchase of the property. Zanker Resource Management was created.

On site, it converted construction debris into usable materials. Concrete and rock was crushed into rock for building roadbeds. Wood debris was crushed to create wood products for burning in hothouse steam plants, wood chips for ground cover material, and sawdust for garden composting additives. They charged a dumping fee for bringing in the debris, and sold the reconstituted material on the way out. What a deal. Not high tech but certainly it satisfied a need.

Being in the right place at the right time comes forward again

In 1989, California passed the California Integrated Waste Management Act (AB 939) that required the diversion of materials from landfills. Local government jurisdictions were required to meet solid waste diversion goals of twenty-five percent by 1995 and fifty percent by 2000. A large percentage of this solid waste material was found to be compostable yard materials such as grass, tree limbs, and wood products of all kinds. Zanker's Z-Best Composting Facility and their Zanker Road Landfill and Resource Recovery Operation processes approximately 1,000 tons of compostable material per day.

In 1991, Zanker created a new business unit, GreenWaste Recovery, that bid for and won a contract with the City of San Jose to collect the yard waste and wood products from over one hundred thousand homes. These tree limbs, leaves, grass clippings, and other wood products were diverted from landfill by processing them at the Zanker's facilities creating compost for landscapers and farmers and wood chips as co-generation fuels.

GreenWaste continued to expand its collection programs to include the pickup of solid waste, recyclable materials and yard trimmings and additional jurisdictions around the south bay area in Santa Clara and Santa Cruz counties. GreenWaste also built a material recovery facility (MRF) to process, market and divert recyclable materials from landfill and transfer the yard trimmings to Zanker's operations. Because neither company owns a landfill that accepts solid waste, both businesses have created sustainable business models to divert material from landfill through successful processing and marketing programs, providing the income stream that had been envisioned in the beginning.

Most recently in 2009 Zanker and GreenWaste formed a new company, Zero Waste Energy Development Company (ZWEDC), to convert the energy rich organic waste into a biogas rich in methane utilizing a high solids anaerobic digestion process. ZWEDC constructed the facility in

2012/2013 and it was the first large-scale commercial facility in the United States and largest in the world when it opened its doors in late 2013. Only time will tell if the process and the company will be successful going forward, but so far all indications are strong.

On to New Ventures... or should I say *Adventures*

Being on my own for the first time in my business career, I looked around for new opportunities.

The acceleration of technology growth during the seventies and through the nineties was extraordinary. Through this book, I have tried to show the evolution of hardware and software and how it has changed the way we communicate and work in just the past thirty or forty years. There were many opportunities waiting to be discovered that would support this incredible high technology growth.

I was getting calls to help new start-ups and they represented opportunities to invest in early stage designs with the possibility of multiplying my investment through their success.

In 1982, a neighbor got approval to start a new bank and asked me to invest. Saratoga National Bank was formed and did very well. A larger bank that increased the value of the investment subsequently acquired it.

Prometheus Products

In 1984, Prometheus Products was another early venture I made into the new world of data communications. They made modulator-demodulators (modems) for this new industry of data communications between remote computer systems. The modem was the means for connecting remote computers across phone lines (remember that this was BEFORE the Internet.) This was a short-lived solution to data communication and Sierra Semiconductor, the supplier of the circuitry used in their design, subsequently bought Prometheus Products. A bit later, a Canadian semiconductor company bought Sierra Semiconductor, part of the consolidation in newly developing industries.

It was at this time that dedicated communication lines were being made available for data and a new industry was quickly becoming a new norm.

Tigan Communications

Recall that Dale Mrazek designed and patented Tri-State Logic at National Semiconductor. In early 1984, I agreed to help him found Tigan Communications to design and build network servers, interface controllers, routers, and switches for transmitting data over dedicated lines, again, before the Internet was created. I helped by writing a business plan and creating marketing documents and managing the sales and marketing functions. Tigan was awarded a contract to build a network server system for the Minnesota Educational Computer Consortium. This system met with some success, but it was subsequently overshadowed by a venture capital-funded company called 3Com. Tigan had too little funding to compete and got overrun.

Productivity Software Inc.

Rupert Lissner created and coded an integrated software program called AppleWorks for the Apple II. The program was one of the first integrated software programs made available on a personal computer. The package included word processing, spreadsheet, drawing, database, and communication applications. At the time, the Internet was not available and computer-to-computer communication was done over a telephone line using a modem for interconnection. The ability to share spreadsheets or word processing documents over the telephone lines, using the communications app in AppleWorks was an amazing success and was of great benefit for Apple II users.

When Apple Computer announced the Macintosh, Lissner elected not to transport the application source code over to the Macintosh environment. Don Williams, a business associate and friend, bought the source code from Rupert and formed Productivity Software Inc. to migrate the Apple II version of the program to the Macintosh. He asked me to join him and manage the business and marketing operations while he managed engineering. He recruited five software engineers who did the program conversion of each application package. Over the next year or so, we completed the task and were ready for the market. We made the business decision that it was too expensive for Productivity Software to set up a sales organization for just one product and began looking for a software distributor.

In our mind, the ideal arrangement would be for Apple to license the product and sell it as part of their stable of applications software. Apple was a natural to make this their premiere productivity tool for the Mac. We prepared a presentation for the Macintosh software team and proposed that they distribute our program, which we called Works. Productivity Software would do the upgrades, bug fixes, and the application manuals and they would distribute it through their sales organization. As an alternative we contemplated offering to sell the technology. They declined both of our offers.

Subsequent to their decision not to license Works as an Apple product, they spun off the in-house Apple software development group to create Claris, a separate software company.

Enter Microsoft

The Microsoft relationship is another story unto itself. To digress a little, Bill Gates and Paul Allen knew that IBM was looking for an operating system for use with their soon-to-be entrant into the personal computer market. They bought an operating system from Seattle Computer Products in the early eighties and created an operating system called MS DOS. They proposed this system to IBM for the soon to be announced IBM PC. IBM elected not to own the rights to the Microsoft operating system and they opted to have a non-exclusive license to MS DOS they called PC DOS. Once the IBM PC was announced in 1981, clone companies began to spring up across the country and Microsoft began promoting and licensing MS DOS to these IBM compatible PC companies. Having been blessed with the IBM name, MS DOS became an industry standard in one form or another.

This wide use of their operating system motivated Microsoft to form a new division to develop applications software. Their main applications included a word processor called Word, a spreadsheet called Excel, and a presentation program called PowerPoint. They were initially introduced on IBM PC platforms. Productivity Software didn't know at the time of our distribution arrangement that they were planning to migrate these applications products to the Macintosh.

After Apple Computer turned down Productivity Software, Don Williams began the process of interviewing software distribution companies to determine which companies had the right sales team in place to distribute and sell our Works program. Bill Gates at Microsoft got wind of it and tracked Don down in New York while he was talking to a potential distribution candidate. He asked Don not to sign a contract for distribution without talking to him first. Those discussions led to an agreement to work with Microsoft on a royalty basis. It seemed like a perfect fit. They had a sales force with knowledge of applications software. Our program – *Works* – fit right into their sales concept. The agreement was similar to our Claris offering; Microsoft would manufacture, market and distribute our product through their sales channels and Productivity Software would do all of the development, software maintenance, upgrades, and write the manual and receive a royalty for every unit sold. Microsoft Works became the largest selling product on the Macintosh for the next five years and accounted for almost one hundred million dollars a year in sales by the late eighties. Unfortunately, the story of Productivity Software Inc. is lost forever since it was not documented prior to Don Williams passing.

As time went on, the Works suite of applications was competing with the Microsoft applications and its success became a competitive problem for them. Our totally integrated product sold for one hundred ninety five dollars while Excel, Word, and PowerPoint individually sold for that amount. Works was outselling the Microsoft programs on the Macintosh by a significant number. In particular, our engineers had created superior technical performance in the spreadsheet program over the Excel spreadsheet and it was cutting into their sales. As time went on, our engineers suspected that there was some comingling of our source code that enhanced their Excel program.

In 1989, Bill Gates made us an *offer we couldn't refuse*. He wanted to buy our company. We declined until he said he could always find a way around our copyrighted code. Message received! Productivity Software was a two-man company and Microsoft had the resources of a corporation, and with a gun to our heads we sold the company to them. In short order, Microsoft cancelled the Works program and announced the Microsoft Office Suite package of software, thus eliminating a competitor to their lucrative applications software business. It was a fun business and a new learning experience.

Portable Energy Products (PEP)

In the late eighties the laptop computer was becoming popular and the biggest drawback to its use was the short battery life. Battery life was limited to four to six hours between charges. This was not long enough to make a cross-country plane flight. Rechargeable battery technology consisted of nickel-cadmium (NiCad) and sealed lead acid in the eighties.

A friend asked me to talk to two engineers who had designed a new kind of packaging for sealed lead acid (SLA) batteries. They reportedly needed management and marketing support. Their design for a new sealed lead acid battery intrigued me. I got enamored with the technology and joined them in forming a company to complete the design and manufacturing of this new packaging concept. I funded the operation for five years and took on the responsibility for sales, marketing and the presidency of the corporation.

PEP had a sealed lead acid (SLA) battery with a patented packaging and assembly process that had much better power densities and a far superior form factor than the existing SLAs on the market. The form factor was a flat rectangular configuration. The battery industry scientists said the process was not doable but the engineers proved that theory wrong and patented the process. The flat, rectangular form factor was also more conducive to use in laptop computers as compared to the traditional round flashlight style battery. The largest cell was approximately 2.5 inches wide by 4 inches long by 0.3 inches thick. It had a power density of approximately twenty watt-hours/pound. This was a thirty to forty percent improvement over existing SLAs and comparable to NiCad batteries. It also had an advantage over NiCad in that it had longer shelf life; it could maintain its charge much longer than the NiCad, months versus weeks.

In 1990, PEP had a customer that converted small Nissan cars to electric cars for the Indonesian market. The car used about 2500 cells/car. They also built electric Pedi cabs for the same market. At the time it seemed crazy and yet today, in 2013, Tesla is doing the exact same thing with lithium-ion batteries. A bad cell can be replaced without replacing the whole battery pack.

Our largest customer, IBM, used these cells for back-up power on memory cards in large data storage applications. Being flat, they didn't take up a card slot like the then present cylindrical cells did.

The optimum manufacturing process was an assembly line process where volume was necessary to create an economic advantage through an automated mass production process. The volume for the product was not sufficient to sustain the company and PEP was sold and became part of a bigger corporation. Through all this, the name was changed to Innergy Power Inc. and the company was subsequently sold to a conglomerate called Ecotality.

The growth of the portable intelligence industry: laptops, cell phones, iPads, and etcetera, created the need for higher power densities. This brought about the development of other superior battery technologies such as nickel-metal hydride and later lithium-ion. Its power density was much greater than the SLA technology and the PEP battery became a niche market product that couldn't generate the volume needed to sustain a profitable manufacturing process.

Endosonics Corp.

I was introduced to – and made an investment in – a new medical equipment company called Endosonics Corporation by one of the venture capitalists that made an investment in PEP. They were developing a medical stent for heart procedures that was new and revolutionary. Once the stent was successfully designed and proven it became a manufacturing process and Tyco International, a manufacturing firm, acquired the company.

Chips and Technologies, Inc.

In 1985, a National Semiconductor and Apple Computer colleague contacted me for some reference information on a potential sales vice president. In the conversation, he asked if I would be interested in investing in their company – Chips and Technologies Inc. (C&T). I liked the products they were manufacturing and the people so I said yes I would. A bit later, they invited me to join their board of directors and I was excited to be a part of yet another growing company and a great opportunity to be a part of the next semiconductor boom without working twelve-hour days. It was also another new learning experience for me – how to lead without being at the head of the charge. Board members can only guide and/or recommend strategic planning and corporate direction, something that was new and foreign to me. I had always been in the middle of the fray. After joining the board, I also learned that the investment I made paid that month's payroll. They were that close to a major meltdown. Fortunately for me, they survived and became a good investment.

Intel was the defacto industry standard for the microprocessor used in the PC industry as this market was exploding. They did not, however, design the interface devices that completed the chip complement needed to make a computer.

Chips & Technologies was founded to design these peripheral components that surrounded the Intel central processor. They had an excellent team of designers proficient in the design of these interface devices: keyboard encoders, video monitor interface, sound, memory controller, etc.

In the late 1980s, fabless semiconductor companies (ones that design microchips but contract out their manufacture), started a major change in the development of semiconductor companies. The cost of building a semiconductor fabrication factory had grown to the hundreds of millions of dollars and was a barrier to the creation of new semiconductor companies. They specialized in the latest process technologies and left the design of new products to companies whose expertise was more in the design of products than in the manufacturing of the semiconductor component. A consortium was formed to push this concept and Chips and Technologies was among the first to join this fabless companies revolution.

A senior manufacturing executive at Texas Instruments, Dr. Morris Chang, started a semiconductor fabrication company in 1987 to manufacture metal-oxide-semiconductor-field-effect transistor (MOSFET) devices to a standard process specification common to the consortium companies. Taiwan Semiconductor Company (TSMC) was initially listed on the Taiwan stock exchange, but in 1997, went public on the New York Stock Exchange (NYSE). This evolution has helped move the technology forward.

As time progressed, the business of Chips and Technologies converged with that of Intel and it became obvious that C&T was in the path of an 800-pound gorilla. As the technology of semiconductor fabrication improved, component count on a chip increased and Intel began to incorporate the peripheral devices on the microprocessor chip. It would require a major investment to redirect the company into other businesses. Management – along with the board – concluded that C&T should approach Intel Executive Vice President Leslie Vadasz about a merger of the two companies and Intel acquired Chips and Technologies in July 1997.

Aldus Corporation

In 1984, I was invited to view a new software application product being evaluated as a possible investment by a venture capital fund. It was a new concept in software for the Macintosh computer. The VC fund members did not know enough about the recently introduced Macintosh to pass judgment on the concept and invited me to come to the meeting and help them evaluate the software. The company was Aldus Corporation and they would change the way page layout documents are created forever.

The creation of Postscript fonts by Adobe Systems and the LaserWriter Printer/Macintosh combination at Apple Computer was about to revolutionize the page layout concept for magazines and newspapers. In 1985, a program called PageMaker was introduced on the Macintosh. An IBM PC compatible version was introduced in 1987.

The founder, Paul Brainerd, had worked for a newspaper in Minnesota and conceived a computer equivalent of the age-old process of typesetting. The Macintosh had the ability to handle the postscript fonts, format a page, along with the insertion of pictures or graphs, and print it out on a LaserWriter printer. There is a documented interview with Paul on the Computer History Museum website.

I was intrigued by the concept and when offered the opportunity to invest in the first round of venture capital, I agreed. I had just walked into an opportunity.

About 1986, I was invited to join the Aldus board and declined because it was in Seattle and I didn't want to travel. A few months later, they made me another offer that I accepted and joined the board. This turned out to be a substantial opportunity. It was an incredible opportunity to learn about a new personal computer software concept that would change the way magazines, brochures, and newspapers are created today. As I said before, I always like to learn new concepts.

The PageMaker program sold for $495 and was a big hit with small business and service organizations that needed a way to put out advertisements and brochures. PageMaker was quickly picked it up by these organizations, which also enhanced the sale of Macintosh computers and LaserWriter printers, another Apple product. However, the price point was substantially higher than most individual users could afford.

I suggested that they use the approach I had learned in the semiconductor business. In the early days of transistors and integrated circuits, the development costs for new technologies and design concepts was borne by the military equipment companies that needed these new components for their next generation designs. As yields improved and the cost of manufacture came down, the components could be priced to sell in the industrial/consumer marketplace where price competition is much more crucial.

The early adopters essentially paid for the development of PageMaker, and Aldus began development of a stripped down version for the home office market. They acquired a consumer/commercial company called Silicon Beach Software and began marketing products for the consumer marketplace, which expanded their reach into a whole new desktop publishing opportunity. Today, it is a staple for anyone that needs page layout and small volume runs of documents.

The Adobe Acquisition of Aldus

As time went on, the CEO Paul Brainerd wanted to back away from day-to-day operations and brought in a chief operating officer. In time, her management style nearly derailed the entire management team. During a company function and a board meeting, it became known to me that several members of the executive staff were getting ready to jump ship. They did not like her style of managing. She came from an old-line company and was not familiar with the fast paced policies of these new entrepreneurial industries. To bring peace among the management, she was asked to resign to keep the management staff intact. After that, Aldus began looking for a new CEO. It is difficult for many entrepreneurs to find someone they feel can do the job as well as them. Paul rejected several prospective candidates and the board recommended that he find a buyer for the company.

In 1994, Adobe Systems acquired Aldus Corporation. PageMaker was a good fit for the Adobe product line. It used the Adobe font library and provided the Aldus page layout process that fit the Adobe Systems applications programs

As part of the merger agreement, Aldus was given two board seats on the Adobe board and I was asked to be one of them.

Adobe Acrobat

When I joined the Adobe board, they were just creating a program that converted all varieties of text files on all varieties of computers into a universally read common format. The application program, called Adobe Acrobat, consisted of a file translator and a reader.

Acrobat could convert these varied files of data into a standard format called a portable document format (PDF). The proprietary Acrobat program could then translate this file into one readable on any computer. This development created a world changing software package that would control the distribution of documents, tantamount to the development of the MS DOS operating system by Microsoft that controlled a large share of the personal computer industry. The Reader is a free program that can read the PDF files created by Acrobat.

At the time, Adobe did not have a strong marketing department. It was obvious they were not properly focused – marketing-wise – to merchandise and take advantage of this incredible new creation. Their marketing was focused on selling the $39 document reader package (Reader) instead of on selling a document translator package (Acrobat) to large corporations and government entities that could make it an industry standard program. I thought it was a great opportunity to make a contribution and spoke up that they were focused on the wrong part of the opportunity. I was excited about this prospect and, at a board meeting, voiced my opinion that they were missing an opportunity to create an industry standard. CEO John Warnock took this as an affront and did not take the comments kindly. As a result, I lost favor with him. One of the board members suggested that they hire me as a marketing consultant to help them out and he said he wasn't interested in doing that. This was a bad mistake on my part for not being more diplomatic. It would have been a great challenge that fit into my skills. The creation of PDF files has successfully taken their place in the world of document transfer and Adobe is doing very well. My tenure on the Aldus/Adobe board spanned almost fourteen years.

Connect, Inc.

Connect, Inc., early in the development of the Internet, created an email application that was very easy to use and had one great feature missing in todays mail programs: it provided feedback when your email had been read. This was useful when important messages were being sent. You knew that it had been received and that it had been read, even if the recipient didn't respond.

Their shortcoming was they didn't address the market of getting companies to set up their email system around the Connect software. Like Adobe, they focused on selling the $39 application to individuals when they needed companies to endorse the concept and make it a company standard. Great engineering without great marketing/sales doesn't always sell a product.

Venture Capital

This period of my working life was a dynamic time in the high technology industry. I knew very little about venture capital as an industry so was doing these investments as a result of personal contacts.

During the growth in high technology start-up companies in the 1970s and 1980s, an industry of investment companies sprang up in Silicon Valley. Populated by a few in the seventies it grew exponentially in the eighties and nineties. Some of the venture capitalists made copious amounts of money and began to be selective in their investments in new start-ups.

The venture capitalists had many opportunities to invest millions of dollars – sometimes hundreds of millions of dollars – in big start-ups with large potential returns. Consequently, they weren't interested in funding companies who needed only a few hundred thousand dollars to get started.

Angel Investing

This created a cottage industry of individual investors to serve early stage financing for companies that needed smaller seed round investments that the large venture capitalists weren't interested in supporting.

The success of the investments that I had made in the various named companies provided me with funds that I could invest in more start-ups. This seemed like a greater more organized opportunity to stay peripherally involved in new and exciting developments. It also gave me a reason to stay current on new technologies, so I joined the new cottage industry of angel investing.

The first group to emerge was called The Band of Angels. The Band of Angels was a group of individual investors that got together once a month for dinner and would invite three or four companies to make a presentation on their company. They presented what business they were in, how much seed money they needed, and who the major key personnel were in the endeavor. If they found enough angel investors interested in their new company, they could get funding to reach the next level of development. This group met for several years until one of the leaders passed away and the members lost interest and the group disbanded.

Another group was called Garage.Com. This was also a forum for angel investors to learn about newly conceived companies looking for seed round funding. Once a month there was a breakfast meeting where the group listened to presentations from early stage companies who would give a twenty-minute presentation on their company plans. Anyone interested would then make an appointment with the company to get more information with which to make a better decision.

Initially, these start-up companies were largely in the development of hardware products. As hardware technology expanded and people became more computer-centric, new applications began to emerge. Cell phones were the hottest new hardware devices being designed and they required new semiconductor concepts such as low power microprocessors and peripherals. Semiconductor development was not just for the phone itself, but also for the communications equipment allowing communication between existing landlines and the new cell phone technology. The cell phone needed to be added to the existing telephone infrastructure through wireless local area networks (LAN) that connected them via transmitting/receiving cell tower networks to provide "anywhere and anytime" communication. Telephone data/voice equipment and communications transmitting networks were needed for worldwide access to the telephone system. A whole new genre of products evolved, the most important of which was the development of the Internet. This created the need for new concepts in software development in order to make cell phones and tablets useful tools – systems software to handle the communications, and applications software to make use of this new communication medium.

The telecommunications explosion brought on by the development of the cell phone and tablet devices created a bigger software/hardware industry than any we had seen before. This, along with the incredible growth in applications we now know as Facebook, Twitter, Maps, Linkedin, and online banking, to name a few, created a whole new business environment in which to participate. A technology research firm predicted that by 2020, over 200 billion Internet linked objects will create $7 billion in sales.

Large portions of these software programs were the vision of one or two entrepreneurs. They required little capital to get started. The angel investments served as seed money for companies that were later funded by the larger venture capital funds as they grew in size.

Over the years, I made numerous investments with varying degrees of success through angel investing.

Examples of new software programs

In the early days of data transmission, it was not uncommon to try and download a large data file, for example, that would take hours because of slow download times and dropped communications. A Berkeley professor – who is an expert on code correction – devised an "on the fly" error correction scheme for transmitted software, making corrections as they occur. His company, Digital Fountain, provided error correction software for packet switching transmission of data over the Internet. Errors in the data packets due to transmission glitches or atmospheric interference would be identified and corrected on-the-fly. It was a godsend to those who relied on data communications of large files. It fell by the wayside as better digital transmission facilities and error correcting alternatives evolved.

Sendmail was the basis for email, as we know it today. It was a free email app that spread like wildfire. It was a quicker alternative to the U.S. Postal Service. Sending mail by way of the U.S. Post Office was called snail mail. The free program spread like wild fire and became very popular. Sendmail tried to monetize this opportunity and make a business out of email transmission, but in 2013 it too fell to better technologies. This was a very fast moving technological time for the data communications industry.

Those and several other investment opportunities in this fast moving genre led me to believe that I wasn't qualified to play in the software sandbox. It required more effort than I was willing to put forth to understand a different technical environment from my training in hardware and semiconductor development. As in any new business venture, you must be committed to it and willing to put in whatever time it takes to make the venture successful. I didn't do that, nor was I willing to. I decided to let the professionals do it and invested in professionally managed venture capital funds from then on. They have been far more successful.

Another new adventure: Presenting a college level Seminar

In the late 1980s, Jennifer Bestor, a young lady who had worked in sales at Apple contacted me with an opportunity to create a college level seminar for Business School students. Jennifer had returned to Stanford University to get her masters degree in Business Administration. She observed that most business school (B school) students were either college postgraduate students or older students that had returned to college to further their education. This group primarily consisted of economics, finance, and manufacturing specialty students who had little or no knowledge of the sales and marketing side of business. She suggested a seminar that would provide insight into how these organizations worked within a company. We put together a two-hour seminar to cover the selling process, marketing and advertising techniques, and business plan development. It was offered to the B School students each winter quarter. It was very satisfying to teach these processes to interested students. I really enjoyed the experience for three years. Unfortunately, the Dean of the Business School, Dr. Robert Davis retired and my stint as a seminar presenter was ended.

Epilogue

I have had the good fortune of being involved with some of this century's greatest innovations, starting with the development of bipolar semiconductor technology in the 1960s and 70s that evolved from a single transistor on a chip of silicon to devices using multiple transistors and passive components, called integrated circuits (ICs). They further evolved into complex circuits on a chip commonly called medium scale integrated circuits (MSI). In the 1970s and 80s, the lower powered MOS or MOSFET device technology was refined and thousands of individual components were put on a single chip and defined as a large scale integrated circuit (LSI). Eventually, LSI devices evolved into very large integrated circuits (VLSI) and memory components.

Advancement in manufacturing capability made possible the creation of a computer on a chip – the microprocessor. This creation started the evolution from a 4-bit computer – made up of about three thousand individual components on a chip of silicon – to a 64-bit multi-core computer chip made up of more than a billion individual components on a silicon chip. In a few short years, the development of the microprocessor advanced computer technology from room-sized mainframes to desktop personal computers. The processing power of the computer in today's cell phone can be compared to the mainframe computers of fifty years ago.

I have also been a part of the development of application software that has changed the way business is conducted. Designing, marketing, selling, and lastly, investing in their development was all part of my working life. In less than a century, we have seen the birth of the most primitive automobile evolve into one that can drive itself. We have seen the development of the airplane evolve from the Wright Brothers primitive glider into spaceships and remote controlled drones. A large part of the evolution came about as the result of the invention of the semiconductor. As I have said before, *Necessity is the mother of invention.*

I only wish I could go back and do it all over again.

WOW! What a Ride.

About the Author

After a stint in the Navy, Carter graduated from the Milwaukee School of Engineering in 1960 and began his career at Sandia Corporation, a research and development facility for the Atomic Energy Commission in Albuquerque, New Mexico. He worked on the development of early stage semiconductor technology for weapons grade electronics. His career went on to semiconductor product marketing at Fairchild Semiconductor and National Semiconductor and then into sales management for personal computers at Apple Computer, Inc. Carter has lived in the Silicon Valley, California for over 50 years.